Applied Reinforcement Learning with Python

With OpenAI Gym, Tensorflow, and Keras

Taweh Beysolow II

Apress®

Applied Reinforcement Learning with Python: With OpenAI Gym,
Tensorflow, and Keras

Taweh Beysolow II
San Francisco, CA, USA

ISBN-13 (pbk): 978-1-4842-5126-3   ISBN-13 (electronic): 978-1-4842-5127-0
https://doi.org/10.1007/978-1-4842-5127-0

Managing Director, Apress Media LLC: Welmoed Spahr
Acquisitions Editor: Celestin Suresh John
Development Editor: Rita Fernando
Coordinating Editor: Divya Modi

Cover designed by eStudioCalamar

Cover image designed by Freepik (www.freepik.com)

Distributed to the book trade worldwide by Springer Science+Business Media New York, 233 Spring Street, 6th Floor, New York, NY 10013. Phone 1-800-SPRINGER, fax (201) 348-4505, e-mail orders-ny@springer-sbm.com, or visit www.springeronline.com. Apress Media, LLC is a California LLC and the sole member (owner) is Springer Science + Business Media Finance Inc (SSBM Finance Inc). SSBM Finance Inc is a **Delaware** corporation.

For information on translations, please e-mail rights@apress.com, or visit http://www.apress.com/rights-permissions.

Apress titles may be purchased in bulk for academic, corporate, or promotional use. eBook versions and licenses are also available for most titles. For more information, reference our Print and eBook Bulk Sales web page at http://www.apress.com/bulk-sales.

Any source code or other supplementary material referenced by the author in this book is available to readers on GitHub via the book's product page, located at www.apress.com/978-1-4842-5126-3. For more detailed information, please visit http://www.apress.com/source-code.

Printed on acid-free paper

This book is dedicated to my friends and family who supported me through the most difficult of times for the past decade. They have enabled me to be the person I am capable of being when operating at my best. Without you, I would not have the ability to continue living as happily as I am.

Table of Contents

About the Author

Taweh Beysolow II is a data scientist and author currently based in the United States. He has a bachelor of science in economics from St. Johns University and a master of science in applied statistics from Fordham University. After successfully exiting the start-up he co-founded, he now is a Director at Industry Capital, a San Francisco–based private equity firm, where he helps lead the cryptocurrency and blockchain platforms.

About the Technical Reviewer

Santanu Pattanayak currently works at GE Digital as a Staff Data Scientist and is author of the deep learning book *Pro Deep Learning with TensorFlow* (Apress, 2017). He has 8 years of experience in the data analytics/data science field and also has a background in development and database technologies. Prior to joining GE, Santanu worked in companies such as RBS, Capgemini, and IBM. He graduated with a degree in electrical engineering from Jadavpur University, Kolkata, and is an avid math enthusiast. Santanu is currently pursuing a master's degree in data science from the Indian Institute of Technology (IIT), Hyderabad. He also devotes his time to data science hackathons and Kaggle competitions where he ranks within the top 500 across the globe. Santanu was born and brought up in West Bengal, India, and currently resides in Bangalore, India, with his wife.

Acknowledgments

I would like to thank Santanu, Divya, Celestin, and Rita. Without you, this book would not be nearly as much of a success as it will be. Secondarily, I would like to thank my family and friends for their continued encouragement and support. Life would not be worth living without them.

Introduction

It is a pleasure to return for a third title with Apress! This text will be the most complex of those I have written, but will be a worthwhile addition to every data scientist and engineer's library. The field of reinforcement learning has undergone significant change in the past couple of years, and it is worthwhile for everyone excited with artificial intelligence to engross themselves in.

As the frontier of artificial intelligence research, this will be an excellent starting point to familiarize yourself with the status of the field as well as the most commonly used techniques. From this point, it is my hope that you will feel empowered to continue on your own research and innovate in your own respective fields.

CHAPTER 1

Introduction to Reinforcement Learning

To those returning from my previous books, *Introduction to Deep Learning Using R*[1] and *Applied Natural Learning Using Python*,[2] it is a pleasure to have you as readers again. To those who are new, welcome! Over the past year, there have continued to be an increased proliferation and development of Deep Learning packages and techniques that revolutionize various industries. One of the most exciting portions of this field, without a doubt, is Reinforcement Learning (RL). This itself is often what underlies a lot of generalized AI applications, such as software that learns to play video games or play chess. The benefit to reinforcement learning is that the agent can familiarize itself with a large range of tasks assuming that the problems can be modeled to a framework containing actions, an environment, an agent(s). Assuming that, the range of problems can be from solving simple games, to more complex 3D games, to teaching self-driving cars how to pick up and drop off passengers in a

---

[1]New York: Apress, 2018.
[2]New York: Apress, 2017.

© Taweh Beysolow II 2019
T. Beysolow II, *Applied Reinforcement Learning with Python*,
https://doi.org/10.1007/978-1-4842-5127-0_1

variety of different places as well as teaching a robotic arm how to grasp objects and place them on top of a kitchen counter.

The implications of well-trained and deployed RL algorithms are huge, as they more specifically seek to drive artificial intelligence outside of some of the narrow AI applications spoken about in prior texts I have written. No longer is an algorithm simply predicting a target or label, but instead is manipulating an agent in an environment, and that agent has a set of actions it can choose to achieve a goal/reward. Examples of firms and organizations which devote much time to researching Reinforcement Learning are Deep Mind as well as OpenAI, whose breakthroughs in the field are among the leading solutions. However, let us give a brief overview of the history of the field itself.

History of Reinforcement Learning

Reinforcement Learning in some sense is a rebranding of optimal control, which is a concept extending from control theory. Optimal control has its origins in the 1950s and 1960s, where it was used to describe a problem where one is trying to achieve a certain "optimal" criterion and what "control" law is needed to achieve this end. Typically, we define an optimal control as a set of differential equations. These equations then define a path toward values that minimize the value of the error function. The core of optimal control is the culmination of Richard Bellman's work, specifically that of dynamic programming. Developed in the 1950s, dynamic programming is an optimization method that emphasizes the solving of a large individual problem by breaking it down into smaller and easier-to-solve components. It is also considered the only feasible method of solving stochastic optimal control problems and moreover consider in general all of optimal control to be reinforcement learning.

Bellman's most notable contribution to optimal control is that of the Hamilton-Jacobi-Bellman (HJB) equation. The HJB equation

$$\dot{V}(x,t) + \min_{u} \{ \nabla V(x,t) \cdot F(x,u) + C(x,u) \} = 0,$$

$$\text{s.t. } V(x,T) = D(X)$$

where $\dot{V}(x,t)$ = the partial derivate of V w.r.t. the time variable t. $a \cdot b$, $\dot{V}(x,t)$ = Bellman value function (unknown scalar) or the cost incurred from starting in state x at time t and controlling the system optimally until time T, C = the scalar cost rate function, D = final utility state function, $x(t)$ = system state vector, $x(0)$ = an assumed given, $u(t)$ for $0 \leq t \leq T$.

The solution yielded from this equation is the value function, or the minimum cost for a given dynamic system. The HJB equation is the standard method by which one solves an optimal control problem. Furthermore, dynamic programming is generally the only feasible way or method for solving stochastic optimal control problems. One of these problems, which dynamic programming was developed to help solve, is Markov decision processes (MDPs).

MDPs and their Relation to Reinforcement Learning

We describe MDPs as discrete time stochastic control process. Specifically, we define discrete time stochastic processes as a random process in which the index variable is characterized by a set of discrete, or specific, values (in contrast to continuous values). MDPs are specifically useful for situations in which outcomes are partially affected by participants in the process but the process also exhibits some degree of randomness as well. MDPs and dynamic programming thus become the basis of reinforcement learning theory.

Plainly stated, we assume based on a Markov property that the future is independent of the past given the present. In addition to this, this state is considered sufficient if it gives us the same description of the future as if we have the entirety of the historical information. This in essence means that the current state is the only piece of information that will be relevant and that all historical information is no longer necessary. Mathematically, a state is said to have the Markov property iff

$$P[S_t + 1 | S_t] = P[S_t + 1 | S_1, \ldots, S_t]$$

Markov processes themselves are considered to be memory-less, in that they are random transitions from state to state. Furthermore, we consider them to be a tuple (S, P) on a state space S where states change via a transition function P, defined as the following:

$$P_{ss'} = \mathbb{P}\,[S_{t+1} = s' | S_t = s],$$

where S = Markov state, S_t = next state.

This transition function describes a probability distribution, where the distribution is the entirety of the possible states that agent can transition to. Finally, we have a reward that we receive from moving from one state to another, which we define mathematically as the following:

$$R_s = \mathbb{E}[R_{t+1} | S_t = S],$$
$$G_t = R_{t+1} + \gamma R_{t+2} + \gamma^2 R_{t+3} + \cdots + \gamma^{k-1} R_{t+k}$$

where γ = discount factor, $\gamma \in [0, 1]$, G_t = total discounted rewards, R = reward function.

We therefore define a Markov reward process (MRP) tuple as (S, P, R, γ).

With all of these formulae now described, the image in Figure 1-1 is an example of a Markov decision process visualized.

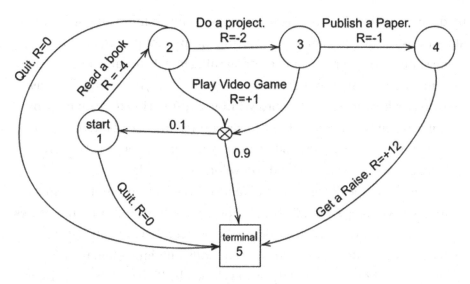

Figure 1-1. *Markov Decision Process*

Figure 1-1 shows how an agent can, with varying probability, move from one state to another, receiving a reward. Optimally, we would learn to choose the process that accumulated the most rewards in a given episode before we failed given the parameters of the environment. This, in essence, is a very basic explanation of reinforcement learning.

Another important component of the development of Reinforcement Learning was trial and error learning, which was one method of studying animal behavior. Most specifically, this has proven useful for understanding basic reward and punishment mechanisms that "reinforce" different behaviors. The words "Reinforcement Learning" however would not appear until the 1960s. During this period, the idea of the "credit-assignment problem" (cap) would be introduced, specifically by Marvin Minsky. Minsky was a cognitive scientist who devoted much of his lifetime to artificial intelligence, such as his book *Perceptrons* (1969) and the paper in which he describes the credit assignment problem, "Steps Toward Artificial Intelligence" (1961). The cap asks how does one distribute "credit" for success with respect to all the decisions that were made in achieving that success. Specifically, many reinforcement learning algorithms are directly devoted to solving this precise problem. With this being stated, however, trial and error learning largely became less popular, as neural network methods (and supervised learning in general) such as innovations forwarded by Bernard Widrow and Ted Hoff took up most of the interest within the field of AI. However, a resurgence of interest in the field is most notable in the 1980s, when temporal difference (TD) learning truly takes wind as well as with the development of Q learning.

TD learning specifically was influenced by, ironically, another aspect of animal psychology that Minsky pointed out as being important. It comes from the idea of two stimuli, a primary Reinforcer that becomes paired with a secondary Reinforcer and subsequently influences behavior. TD learning itself, however, was largely developed by Richard S. Sutton. He is considered to be one of the most influential figures in the field of RL as his doctoral thesis introduced the idea of temporal credit assignment. This refers to how rewards, particularly in very granular state-action spaces, can be delayed. For example, winning a game of chess requires many actions before one has achieved the "reward" of winning the game. As such, reward signals do not have significant effect on temporally distant states. As such, temporal credit assignment solves for how you reward these granular actions in such a way that meaningfully affect temporally distant states. Q learning, named for the "Q" function that yields the reward, builds on some of these innovations and focuses on finite Markov decision processes.

With Q learning, this brings us to the present day, where further improvements on reinforcement learning are continually being made and represent the bleeding edge of AI. With this overview being complete, however, let us more specifically discuss what readers can be expected to learn.

Reinforcement Learning Algorithms and RL Frameworks

Reinforcement learning analogously is very similar to the domain of supervised learning within traditional machine learning, although there are key differences. In supervised learning, there is an objective answer that we are training the model to predict correctly, whether that is a class label or a particular value, based on the input features from a given observation(s). Features are analogous to the vectors within the given state of an environment, which we feed to the reinforcement learning algorithm typically either as a series of states or individually from one state to the next. However, the main difference is that there is not necessarily always one "answer" to solve the particular problem, in that there are possibly multiple ways by which a reinforcement learning algorithm could successfully solve a problem. In this instance, we obviously want to choose the answer that we can arrive at quickest that simultaneously solves the problem in as efficient a manner as possible. This is precisely where our choice of model becomes critical.

In the prior overview of the history of RL, we introduced several theorems which you will be walked through in detail in the following chapters. However, being that this is an applied text, theory must also be supplied alongside examples. As such, we will be spending a significant amount of time in this text discussing the RL framework OpenAI Gym and how it interfaces with different Deep Learning Frameworks. OpenAI Gym is a framework that allows us to easily deploy, compare, and test Reinforcement Learning algorithms. However, it does have a great degree of flexibility, in that we can utilize Deep Learning methods alongside OpenAI gym, which we will do in our various proofs of concepts. The following shows some simple example code that utilizes the package and the plot that shows the video yielded from the training process (Figure 1-2).

```python
import gym

def cartpole():
    environment = gym.make('CartPole-v1')
    environment.reset()
    for _ in range(50):
        environment.render()
        action = environment.action_space.sample()
        observation, reward, done, info = environment.
        step(action)
        print("Step {}:".format(_))
        print("action: {}".format(action))
        print("observation: {}".format(observation))
        print("reward: {}".format(reward))
        print("done: {}".format(done))
        print("info: {}".format(info))
```

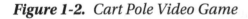

Figure 1-2. *Cart Pole Video Game*

When reviewing the code, we notice that when working with gym, we must initialize an environment in which our algorithms sit. Although it is common to work with environments provided by the package, we can also create our own environments for custom tasks (like video games not provided by gym). Moving forward however, let us discuss the other variables defined worth noting as shown from the terminal output as follows.

```
action: 1
observation: [-0.02488139  0.00808876  0.0432061   0.02440099]
reward: 1.0
done: False
info: {}
```

The variables can be broken down as follows:

- **Action** – Refers to action taken by the agent within an environment that subsequently yields a reward

- **Reward** – Yielded to the agent. Indicates the quality of action with respect to accomplishing some goal

- **Observation** – Yielded by the action: Refers to the state of the environment after an action has been performed

- **Done** – Boolean that indicates whether the environment needs to be reset

- **Info** – Dictionary with miscellaneous information for debugging

The process flow that describes the actions is shown in Figure 1-3.

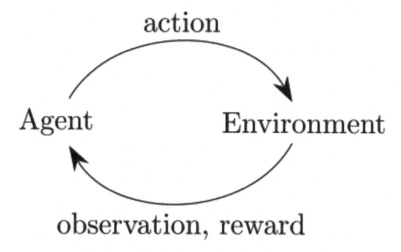

Figure 1-3. *Process Flow of RL Algorithm and Environment*

To provide more context, Figure 1-2 shows a cart and a pole video game, where the objective is to successfully balance the cart and the pole such that the pole never tilts over. As such, a reasonable objective would be to train some DL or ML algorithm such that we can do this. We will tackle this particular problem later in the book however. The purpose of this section is just to briefly introduce OpenAI Gym.

Q Learning

We briefly discussed Q learning in the introduction; however, it is worthwhile to highlight the significant portion of this text we will utilize to discuss this topic. Q learning is characterized by the fact that there is some police, which informs an agent of the actions to take in different scenarios. While it does not require a model, we can use one, and it specifically is often applied for finite Markov decision processes. Specifically, the variants we will tackle in this text are Q learning, Deep Q Learning (DQL), and Double Q Learning (Figure 1-4).

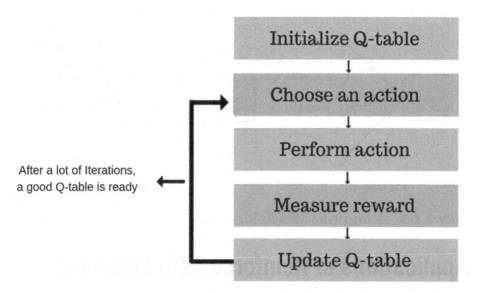

Figure 1-4. Q Learning Flow Chart

We will discuss this more in depth in the chapters that specifically reference these techniques; however, Q learning and Deep Q Learning each have respective advantages given the complexity of the problem, while both often suffering from similar downfalls.

Actor-Critic Models

The most advanced of the models we will be tackling in this book are the Actor-Critic Models, which are comprised of the A2C and A3C. Both of these respectively stand for Advantage Actor-Critic and Asynchronous Advantage Actor-Critic models. While both of these are virtually the same, the difference is that the latter has multiple models that work alongside each other and update the parameters independently while the former updates its parameters for all of the models simultaneously. These models update on a more granular basis (action to action) rather than in an episodic manner as many of the other Reinforcement Learning algorithms do. Figure 1-5 shows an example of the Actor-Critic Models visualized.

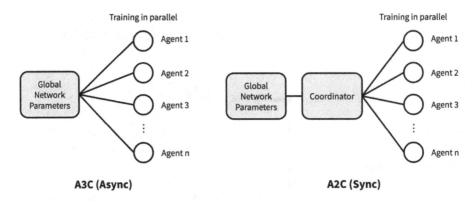

Figure 1-5. *Actor-Critic Models Visualized*

Applications of Reinforcement Learning

After the reader has been thoroughly introduced to the concepts of reinforcement learning, we will tackle multiple problems where the focus will be showing the reader how to deploy solutions that we will be training and utilizing on cloud environments.

Classic Control Problems

Being that the field of optimal control has been around for roughly the past 60 years, there are a handful of problems that we will begin tackling first that users will see often referenced in other reinforcement learning literature. One of them is the cart pole problem, which is referenced in Figure 1-2. This is a game in which the user is required to try and balance a cart pole using the optimal set of options. Another one of these is shown in Figure 1-6, called Frozen Lake, in which the agent learns how to cross a lake which is frozen without stepping on the ice that would cause the agent to fall through.

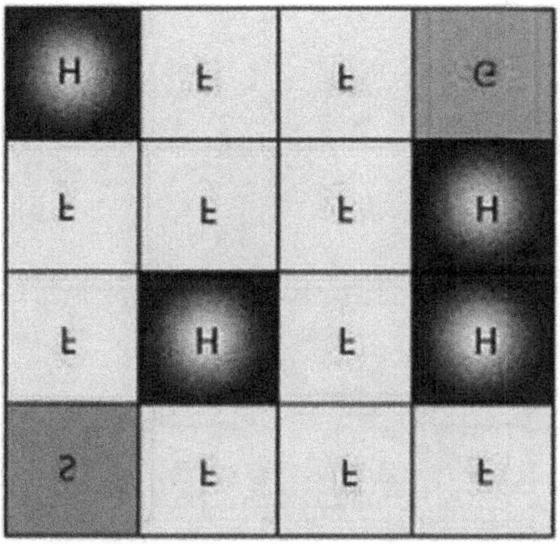

Figure 1-6. *Frozen Lake Visualized*

Super Mario Bros.

One of the most beloved video games of all time turns out to be one of the best ways to display how the use of reinforcement learning in artificial intelligence can be applied to virtual environments. With the help of the py_nes library, we are able to emulate *Super Mario Bros.* (Figure 1-7) and then utilize the data from the game such that we can train the model to play the level. We will focus on one level exclusively and will be utilizing AWS resources for this application, giving readers an opportunity to gain experience in this task.

Figure 1-7. *Super Mario Bros.*

Doom

A classic reinforcement learning example that we will apply here is learning to play a simple level of the video game *Doom* (Figure 1-8). Originally released in the 1990s on the PC, the focus of this video game is to successfully kill all the demons and/or enemies you face while making it through the entirety of the level. However, this makes for an excellent application of Deep Q Learning given the scope of actions, the packages available, among other helpful attributes.

Figure 1-8. *Doom Screenshot*

Reinforcement-Based Marketing Making

A common strategy for different proprietary trading firms is to make money by providing liquidity to participants with the objective of buying and selling an asset at any given price. While there are established techniques for this strategy, this is an excellent arena to apply reinforcement learning to as the objectives are relatively straightforward and it is a data-rich field. We will be working with limit order book data from Lobster, a web site which contains a large amount of excellent order book data for experiments such as this. In Figure 1-9, we can see what an example of an order book would look like.

SPDR S&P 500 ETF TR TR UNIT

Orders Accepted	Total Volume
1,153,586	7,689,062

TOP OF BOOK		LAST 10 TRADES		
SHARES	PRICE	TIME	PRICE	SHARES
11,000	180.07	14:42:13	180.03	100
12,500	180.06	14:42:11	180.02	100
12,900	180.05	14:42:11	180.01	100
9,700	180.04	14:42:09	180.01	100
1,100	180.03	14:42:09	180.01	200
6,400	180.02	14:42:08	180.01	100
9,700	180.01	14:42:06	180.01	100
9,600	180.00	14:42:06	180.01	100
14,700	179.99	14:42:06	180.01	100
11,500	179.98	14:42:06	180.01	100

(ASKS: rows 180.07–180.03; BIDS: rows 180.02–179.98)

Figure 1-9. Limit Order Book

Sonic the Hedgehog

Another classic video game that is appropriate for us to utilize different models on will be *Sonic the Hedgehog* (Figure 1-10). Except in this particular chapter, we will walk the reader through the process of creating their own environment from scratch that they can wrap an environment utilizing OpenAI gym and custom software, and then training their own Reinforcement Learning algorithm to then solve the problem of the level. This again will utilize AWS resources for training, piggybacking off of the same processes that were utilized in the other video game examples, specifically *Super Mario Bros.*

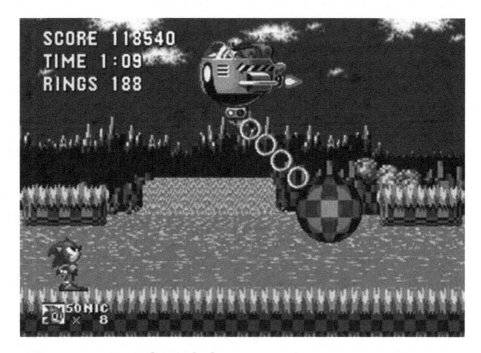

Figure 1-10. *Sonic the Hedgehog*

Conclusion

The purpose of this text will be to familiarize readers with how to apply
Reinforcement Learning in the various contexts that they work in. Readers
should be familiar with Deep Learning Frameworks such as Tensorflow
and Keras, from which we will be working to deploy many of the Deep
Learning models used in conjunction with. While we will take time to
explain reinforcement learning theory, and some of that which overlaps
with Deep Learning might be explained, the majority of this text will be
dedicated to discussing theory and application of RL. With that being said,
let us begin by discussing the basics of Reinforcement Learning in depth.

CHAPTER 2

Reinforcement Learning Algorithms

Readers should be aware that we will be utilizing various Deep Learning and Reinforcement Learning methods in this book. However, being that our focus will shift to discussing implementation and how these algorithms work in production settings, we must spend some time covering the algorithms themselves more granularly. As such, the focus of this chapter will be to walk the reader through several examples of Reinforcement Learning algorithms that are commonly applied and showing them in the context of utilizing OpenAI gym with different problems.

OpenAI Gym

Before we dive into any concrete examples, let's first briefly discuss the software that the reader will be utilizing for the majority of this text. OpenAI is a research institute based in the San Francisco Bay Area. Of the many papers that they have contributed within the field of Artificial Intelligence, one of the greatest open source contributions they have made is the OpenAI "gym." A package released for python, OpenAI gym provides several environments in which users can begin utilizing reinforcement learning algorithms. We will utilize this package most specifically for the video game environments in which we can train our algorithms; however, let us start by trying to understand the package and how to utilize it.

© Taweh Beysolow II 2019
T. Beysolow II, *Applied Reinforcement Learning with Python*,
https://doi.org/10.1007/978-1-4842-5127-0_2

The basis of gym is the environment. In Chapter 1 we discussed the environment, the various variables we defined, as well as the outputs from the environment. In each game or environment we make, they will often be observed to be different. The cart pole game we play in this chapter will be a very small vector; however, the Super Mario Bros. environment we work through later will be significantly more complex. However, let us start this chapter by looking at the cart pole as well as a new environment and trying to understand what precisely we might want to do within this to solve the problem. The cart pole problem was described by Barto, Sutton, and Anderson (1983) in "Neuronlike Adaptive Elements That Can Solve Difficult Learning Control Problem." The objective in the cart pole problem is to keep the pole balanced on the cart. We receive a reward of 1 for every frame in which the pole is vertical; however, the game is lost if the pole no longer remains vertical in any given frame. We will, instead of focusing on the methods they took to solve this problem, however, focus on utilizing policy gradient methods, one of the bedrocks of Reinforcement Learning.

Policy-Based Learning

Policy-based gradient methods focus on optimizing the policy function directly rather than trying to learn a value function that would yield information on the expected rewards in a given state. Simply stated, we are selecting an action separately from choosing to utilize a value function. Policies bifurcate into the following classes:

- **Deterministic** – A policy that maps a given state to an action(s), specifically where the actions taken "determine" what the outcome will be. For example, you are typing on a keyboard on a word file. When you press "y," you are certain the character "y" will appear on the screen.

- **Stochastic** – A policy that yields a probability distribution over a set of actions, such that there is a probability that the action taken will **not** be the action that occurs. This is specifically used in instances where the environment is **not** deterministic and is an example of a partially observable Markov decision process (POMDP).

Policy-based methods have a few specific advantages over value-based methods, which are important to keep in mind for the reader during the modeling process. Foremost, they tend to converge better on solutions than value-based methods. The reason behind this is that we are being guided toward a solution by a gradient. Intuitively, gradient methods point toward the steepest function we are differentiating. When applied to an error function, and used in the form of gradient descent, we will adjust our actions that minimize the error function's value (locally or globally). As such, we are generally going to have a feasible solution. In contrast, value-based methods can yield a considerably larger and more non-intuitive range of values between actions of minimal difference. Specifically, we do not have the same guarantee of convergence.

Secondly, policy gradients are particularly adept at learning stochastic processes whereas value-based functions cannot. While not every environment is not stochastic, many practical examples of where Reinforcement Learning might hopefully be applied will be stochastic. The reasoning behind why value functions fail here is that they require explicitly defined environments where actions inside of them will yield specific outcomes that must be deterministic. As such, an environment which is stochastic does not have to yield the same outcome for the same action taken, and as such this makes value-based learning in such an environment a null method. In contrast, policy-based methods **do not** need to explore an environment by taking the same action. Specifically, there is no exploration/exploitation trade-off (choosing between what does where the outcome is known vs. trying an action whose outcome is not known). Thirdly, policy-based methods are significantly more effective in high-dimensional spaces, because they are significantly less computationally expensive. Value-based methods require that we calculate a value for each possible action. If we have a space with a considerably high number of actions (or infinite), this will make converging on a solution practically impossible. Policy-based methods just have us perform an action and adjust the gradient. Now that we have a general understanding of policy-based learning methods, let us apply this to the cart pole problem.

Policy Gradients Explained Mathematically

With a broad understanding of policy-based methods, let's dive head first into the mathematical explanation of policy gradients. You should recall in the first chapter that we briefly introduced the concept of Markov decision processes. We define an MDP as a tuple (S, P, R, γ) such that

$$R_s = \mathbb{E}[R_{t+1}|S_t = S],$$

$$G_t = R_{t+1} + \gamma R_{t+2} + \gamma^2 R_{t+3} + \cdots + \gamma^{k-1} R_{t+k}$$

With the reward and the value function defined, we can now mathematically discuss the policy. The environment itself an agent cannot control; however, the agent does have control over what actions it makes, within some bound of reason. As such, the policy is defined as the probability distribution of all actions during a given state of the environment. This is mathematically described as the following:

$$\pi\left(A_t = a|S_t = s\right),$$

$$\forall A_t \in A\left(s\right), S_t \in S$$

where π = the policy, S = state space, A = action space, A_t = action at timestep t, S_t = state at timestep t.

Now, we understand that a policy guides our agent through an environment, where certain actions are possible at a given state that our environment is in. How and where exactly does the policy gradient fit in? The purpose of the policy gradient method is to maximize the expected reward assuming the agent has a policy. The policy therefore is parameterized by θ, where trajectory is defined as τ. Trajectory is broadly defined as the sequences of actions, rewards, and states that we observe over the course of a given episode when we follow a given policy. Episodes themselves refer to instances in which the agent is still performing some set of actions in the environment before we have reached a point where either we have reached the objective of the problem or we have failed the episode entirely. Therefore, the total reward is mathematically defined as $r(\tau)$ such that

$$\arg\max\ J(\theta) = \mathbb{E}_{\pi}\left[r(\tau)\right]$$

We then apply the standard machine learning approach, where we find the best parameters to maximize the policy gradients through gradient descent. As a brief review, the gradient of a function represents the point of greatest rate of increase in the function, and its magnitude is the slope of the graph in that direction. The gradient is usually multiplied by a learning rate, which determines the speed of convergence toward an optimal solution for the function. Simply stated, however, the gradient is typically defined as the first derivative of a given function. How do we utilize this however to optimize a policy choice?

Gradient Ascent Applied to Policy Optimization

Gradient descent–based optimization is common in different machine learning methods, such as linear regression as well as backpropagation for weight optimization in multilayer perceptrons. However, gradient ascent is what we will utilize here to optimize the policy we choose. Instead of trying to minimize the error, we are trying to *maximize* the score that we get over the entirety of the episode that our algorithm will be utilized in. As such, the parameter update should look like the following:

$$\theta := \theta + \alpha \nabla_\theta J(\theta)$$

So the objective of the problem can be stated as the following:

$$\theta^* = \arg \max_\theta E_{\pi\theta}\left[\sum_t R(s_t, a_t)\right]$$

Verbally, we are trying to pick the value of the parameters that maximizes the reward yielded for actions taken within a given state. In the particular instance that we are modeling, we are trying to pick the weights for the network that maximizes the score. We therefore mathematically define the derivative of the expected total reward as the following:

$$\nabla E_\pi\left[r(\tau)\right] = E_\pi\left[r(\tau)\nabla \log \pi(\tau)\right],$$

$$\pi(\tau) = P(s_0)\prod_{t=1}^{T}\pi_\theta\left(a_t|s_t\right)p\left(s_{t+1}, r_{t+1} \mid s_t, a_t\right)$$

The reasoning behind why we take the geometric sum is because, according to the theorems laid forth in Chapter 1 on Markov decision processes, each of the actions taken are independent from one another.

Therefore, the associated cumulative rewards should be calculated in a similar fashion. This process is repeated over the length of the trajectory, which logically follows the length of a given episode and the associated rewards, states, and actions. When we take the log of the total reward, we define that mathematically as the following:

$$\log \pi (\tau) = \log P(s_0) + \sum_{t=1}^{T} \log \pi_\theta (a_t|s_t) + \sum_{t=1}^{T} \log p(s_{t+1}, r_{t+1}|s_t, a_t),$$

$$\nabla \log \pi (\tau) = \sum_{t=1}^{T} \nabla \log \pi_\theta (a_t|s_t) \rightarrow \nabla \mathbb{E}_\pi \left[r(\tau) \right]$$

$$= \mathbb{E}_\pi \left[r(\tau) \left(\sum_{t=1}^{T} \nabla \log \pi_\theta (a_t|s_t) \right) \right]$$

Decomposing all of this, the log of the expected reward is simply the cumulative sum of the log of each of the individual rewards that the policy yields from an action at a given time, given a state, summed over the entirety of the trajectory. The importance of understanding this and what is often referred to as "model-free" algorithms that we utilize in RL is that implicitly shown in these equations is the fact that we never model the environment, because we never know the distribution of the states at all. The only thing that we are modeling, in fact, are the rewards. Now with the mathematical underpinning of policy gradients explained, let us move on next to applying this on a classic control problem: cart pole.

Using Vanilla Policy Gradients on the Cart Pole Problem

For this problem, we will be utilizing Keras, a library known for its ability to quickly deploy neural network models. Although we will utilize Tensorflow later in this chapter, the models we will deploy here will be a part of packages that are defined within the "applied_rl_python/neural_ networks/models.py" file. In here, users will see classes that I have created that will make using these solutions both within and outside of this text easier than defining these architectures repetitively:

```python
class MLPModelKeras():
(Code redacted, please see the source code

    def create_policy_model(self, input_shape):
        input_layer = layers.Input(shape=input_shape)
        advantages = layers.Input(shape=[1])
        hidden_layer = layers.Dense(n_units=self.n_units,
        activation=self.hidden_activation)(input_layer)
        output_layer = layers.Dense(n_units=self.n_columns,
        activation=self.output_activation)(hidden_layer)

        def log_likelihood_loss(actual_labels, predicted_
        labels):
            log_likelihood = backend.log(actual_labels *
            (actual_labels - predicted_labels) + (1 - actual_
            labels) * (actual_labels - predicted_labels))
            return backend.mean(log_likelihood * advantages,
            keepdims=True)

        policy_model = Model(inputs=[input_layer, advantages],
        outputs=output_layer)

        policy_model.compile(loss=log_likelihood_loss,
        optimizer=Adam(self.learning_rate))
        model_prediction = Model(input=[input_layer],
        outputs=output_layer)
        return policy_model, model_prediction
```

What users should take away from this section of code is the fact that we are defining a neural network to be used for policy gradient methods, specifically here one that can be reused and redefined in other problems moving forward. The benefit of Keras is that it allows you to quickly create neural network models that would be significantly more verbose if you had utilized Tensorflow. This additional layer of abstraction automates and reduces the amount of code that needs to be written to write that same neural network model in Keras. In so far as this model is used to solve this specific problem, users should look at Figure 2-1 to try and understand the problem we are trying to solve with this neural network.

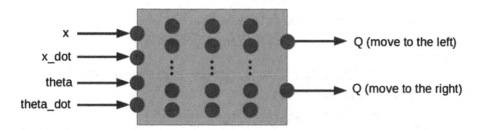

Figure 2-1. *Neural Network for Cart Pole Problem*

The input layer represents the environment and its orientation at that given state, and the two classes represent the probabilities for the respective actions we can take. Specifically, we will choose the action with the highest probability of being correct, as this is modeled as a classification problem.

Moving forward, let us look at the actual code we will be utilizing to solve the problem, found in "chapter2/cart_pole_example.py." This file begins by defining some parameters that are useful to take note of. Although gym is frequently updated, this book was written using gym version 0.10.5. In this particular version, I suggest that readers always define the environment variable globally and later accessing the environment's attributes within different functions. In addition to that, defining the "environment_dimension" variable here resets the environment initially. Now, let us direct our attention to the "cart_pole_game()" function, which is where the majority of the computation will be occurring within this example. Specifically, let us look at the body of the code that continues while we have still not lost the game within a specific episode:

```python
state = np.reshape(observation, [1, environment_
dimension])
prediction = model_predictions.predict([state])[0]
action = np.random.choice(range(environment.action_
space.n), p=prediction)
states = np.vstack([states, state])
actions = np.vstack([actions, action])

observation, reward, done, info = environment.step(action)
reward_sum += reward
rewards = np.vstack([rewards, reward])
```

The beginning of the code should look familiar to readers from the example file given in the first chapter; however, there are some slight differences. We define an observation variable here, which to begin every experiment is the initialized state of the environment. The prediction the model yields are the probabilities. The specific action we take here is a random sample of the possible actions we can take. The states and actions are then appended to a vector which we will utilize later. As usual, we then perform an action within the given environment that yields the new observation, the current reward, as well as an indication as to whether we have failed or are still succeeding within the environment. This process continues until we have lost the game, which brings us to the "calculated_discounted_reward()" function.

What Are Discounted Rewards and Why Do We Use Them?

As stated earlier, the purpose of policy gradient methods is to utilize gradient-based optimization to choose a set of actions that achieve the optimal result in the environment given our objectives. We define the probability distribution of actions that we can take at a given state as the following:

$$\pi_\theta (a|s) = P[a|s]$$

where π = policy, θ = parameter, a = action, s = *state*.

Being that this is a gradient-based optimization problem, we also want to define the cost function, given by the following:

$$J(\theta) = E_{\pi\theta}\left[\Sigma \gamma r\right]$$

The above equation is the policy score function, which is the expected/ average reward of the policy we choose. Because this is an episodic-based task, we suggest that the user calculate the discounted reward on the entire episode. An example of how this is calculated is given by the following equation:

$$J_1(\theta) = E_\pi \left[G_1 = R_1 + \gamma R_2 + \gamma^2 R_3 + \cdots + \gamma^{k-1} R_k \right]$$

$$J_1(\theta) = E_\pi \left(V(s_1) \right)$$

where k = number of steps in episode, G = summed discounted reward, γ = discount tuning parameter, R = reward, V = value.

The calculate_discounted_reward() function gives a vector of the discounted reward for every given reward yielded, and then with the vector reversed, shown as follows:

```
def calculate_discounted_reward(reward, gamma=gamma):
output = [reward[i] * gamma**i for i in range(0, len(reward))]
return output[::-1]
```

We discount the rewards given the value of some tuning parameter that we raise to a different power over each step, and the reward being what is yielded from the environment given the action we take at that step. We then average the discounted rewards vector, which yields the output of the cost function for that episode.

```
discounted_rewards -= discounted_rewards.mean()
discounted_rewards /= discounted_rewards.std()
discounted_rewards = discounted_rewards.squeeze()
```

Readers will observe the following transformations that we perform to the "discounted_rewards" vector. For readers who don't know, the np.array.squeeze() function takes an array with multiple elements and concatenates them such that the following is true:

$$[[1, 2], [2, 3]] \rightarrow [1, 2, 2, 3]$$

The reasoning behind discounted rewards is fairly straightforward in that by discounting rewards, we make an otherwise infinite sum finite. If we do not discount rewards, the sum of these rewards would grow infinitely and therefore we would not be able to converge upon an optimal solution.

How do we calculate the score?

In our code, we specifically utilize the "score_model()" function, which runs a user-specified number of trials using the trained model to yield the average score over these number of trials. This allows us to see, in a generalized sense, how the model is performing, rather than looking at one trial in which the model might have performed better due to chance. Our score function can alternatively be defined as the following:

$$J(\theta) = E_\pi \left[R(\tau) \right]$$

where $R(\tau)$ = expected future reward.

How this is implemented is fairly straightforward; however, let us explain the score_model() function shown as follows:

```
def score_model(model, n_tests, render=render):
(code redacted, please see github)
            state = np.reshape(observation, [1, environment_
            dimension])
            predict = model.predict([state])[0]
            action = np.argmax(predict)
            observation, reward, done, _ = environment.
            step(action)
            reward_sum += reward
            if done:
                break
        scores.append(reward_sum)
    environment.close()
    return np.mean(scores)
```

You will observe that we will not render the environment standard for every time we want to score the model. I recommend this to readers as this significantly would slow the training process in addition to being relatively uninformative. If you do care to render the model, you should only do so once you have a model you feel has reached your benchmarks for a given problem.

In this function, we pass through a model, which we train on a batch earlier. This model is trained specifically utilizing the states and their respective discounted rewards, along with the respective actions we have taken in each of the states. Intuitively, we are trying to train a model to become more accurate at predicting how to predict the actions that would lead to a specific set of rewards by choosing a random action over each iteration. As such, the weights will optimize to yielding the reward given the state consistently. Over time, this should produce a model that when given a specific state will understand what specifically it would do in order to yield a given reward. Therefore, per the framing of the problem, we will eventually yield a model that will yield our score threshold because the weights are optimized to classify a state correctly for the goal of maximizing our score over time.

As with all gradient descent/ascent problems, we have to differentiate the objective function so we can calculate the gradient which is therefore utilized to optimize the weights. Because we are differentiating a probability function, it is recommended that we utilize a logarithm (this is why we utilize a log-likelihood loss for the error function defined on the backend in neural_networks/models.py). Let us look at the plot of a likelihood function vs. the log likelihood of that function (Figures 2-2 and 2-3).

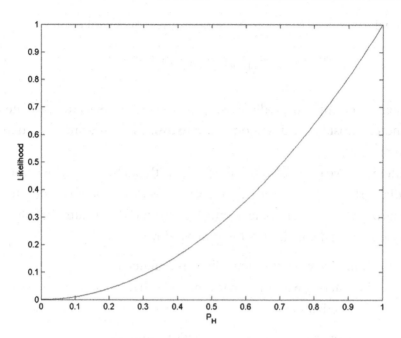

Figure 2-2. *Likelihood Function*

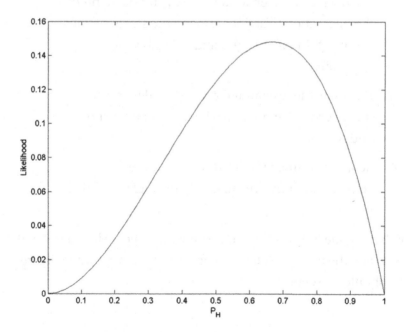

Figure 2-3. *Log-Likelihood Function*

The derivative of the score function is given by the following:

$$\nabla_\theta J(\theta) = E_\pi \Big[\nabla_\theta \big(log\pi(s,a,\theta)\big)R(\tau)\Big] \tag{2.8}$$

Because of utilizing gradient ascent, we are most likely to move the parameters most in the direction that **maximizes** the reward yielded from the environment.

After we have updated our parameters with batch training, we must re-initialize the states, actions, and rewards vectors as being empty. To summarize what the cart_pole_game() function is doing, after having discussed this in detail, here is the process flow:

1. Initialize variables that will be populated by interacting with the environment in their respective states.

2. In a given episode, perform actions until the game has been lost. Given a state, use the model to predict the best action to action. Append the states, actions taken within those states, and rewards yielded in that state.

3. Calculate the discounted rewards and then use those rewards to train on a batch of states, actions, and rewards.

4. Score the trained model and repeat until convergence on performance threshold determined by user.

With our code fully explained, we now can execute it and watch the results. When the user executes the code, the results shown in Figures 2-4 and 2-5 should be seen.

```
Episode: 50
Average Reward: 2.56
Score: 105.6
Error: 0.003579548

Episode: 100
Average Reward: 2.12
Score: 102.8
Error: 0.003846483

Episode: 150
Average Reward: 1.96
Score: 132.2
Error: 0.0039551817
```

Figure 2-4. *Example Output from Policy Gradient Problem*

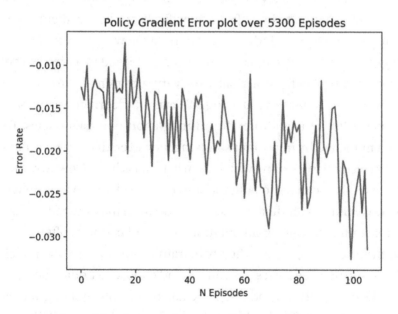

Figure 2-5. *Error Plot from Policy Gradient Problem*

This specific solution converged in approximately 5000–6000 episodes over multiple experiments, with our goal set at 190. We have now completed an example of an episodic problem and one in a discrete problem space. Now that we know the type of problems we can utilize vanilla policy gradients in, where would it be the case that we could not utilize policy gradients?

Drawbacks to Policy Gradients

One of the larger criticisms of reinforcement learning worth addressing at this stage is the sampling efficiency of policy gradients and in RL at large. Sampling efficiency refers to the degree to which our algorithm is able to learn more quickly by only using the states that yield the most important information to learn from. Specifically, policy gradients do not discriminate between the individual actions taken within an episode. Meaning, if the actions we took during an episode lead to a high reward, even if some subset of these actions were very suboptimal, we conclude that those set of actions were all good. We can only learn how to choose an optimal policy by usually iterating through non-optimal policies. This has been mitigated by important sampling; however, that is a technique utilized in off-policy learning which we will discuss later. However, this drawback is not exclusive to policy gradients. In addition to this, policy gradients can have a tendency to converge on local maxima rather than a global maximum as many gradient descent–based methods often can. This also contributes to a greater difficulty in training an appropriate model. To solve some of these issues, we can instead choose to update on a more granular level than the episodic scheme taken in vanilla policy gradients as shown previously. This leads us to our next topic, Proximal Policy Optimization.

Proximal Policy Optimization (PPO) and Actor-Critic Models

PPO specifically deals with policy gradient tendencies to get stuck in local maxima by imposing a penalty on the objective function and then utilizing gradient descent on this newly reformed gradient descent. Such that the equation looks like the following:

$$\max_{\theta} \widehat{\mathbb{E}}_t \left[\frac{\pi_\theta(a_t|s_t)}{\pi_{\theta_{old}}(a_t|s_t)} \widehat{A}_t \right] - \beta \widehat{\mathbb{E}}_t \left[KL \left[\pi_{\theta_{old}}(\cdot|s_t), \pi_\theta(\cdot|s_t) \right] \right] \qquad (2.9)$$

where β = tuning parameter, KL = KL divergence, $\widehat{A}_t$ = advantage function.

The basic intuition behind this adaptive penalty is that we utilize the KL divergence between the old and the new policy, which will change over each iteration within an episode. If the value from the KL divergence is higher than the target value δ, we shrink the tuning parameter. However, if it falls below the target value δ, we expand the region in which we are willing to search for different parameters. The benefit to adding the penalty is that it ensures that the area in which we search for the parameters to define the policy is significantly smaller and adjusts based on the degree of correctness on a much more granular level than episodic. That way, bad actions within an episode will be penalized directly rather than being averaged out across other decisions that might have been good. This stepwise rather than episodic change is the key component to the Actor-Critic model, on which PPO is based. In this instance, the tuning parameter tied with the KL divergence is the critic model with the policy being the actor.

The advantage function will be a key component of Actor-Critic models, which we utilize instead of a value function to the algorithm's decision-making process. The reasoning here is because value functions have high variability, whereas advantage functions more clearly convex functions. The intuition behind how the gradient optimization is that our parameters will optimize in directions where the advantage function is above 0 and will move away from parameter choices where gradients are below 0. Next, we define the advantage function which we will utilize instead of a value function:

$$A(s,a) = Q(s,a) - V(s)$$

where $Q(s, a)$ = Q value for action a in state s, $V(s)$ = average value of states s.

Actor-Critic models bifurcate into two strategies: (1) Actor Advantage Critic (A2C) and (2) Asynchronous Advantage Actor-Critic (A3C). Both of these algorithms work as we have briefly described Actor-Critic models; however, the only difference is that A3C does not update the global parameters for every actor at the same time (at the end of every iteration), hence the asynchronous description. The training will be faster for A2C in this instance.

Let us inspect this algorithm more closely, however, by applying it to a slightly more difficult game than cart pole, Super Mario Bros, and solving the solution more directly.

Implementing PPO and Solving Super Mario Bros.

For this model, we will be utilizing code that is provided within some of the packages that I have created as well as open source libraries. Although the game can be changed, users should also feel free to try and solve this problem utilizing other problems. Because of the training time that is associated with A3C, I am going to utilize A2C. In addition to this, I will briefly walk users through how to set up a Google Cloud instance for training, which is recommended for any reinforcement learning–based task such as this.

Overview of Super Mario Bros.

Super Mario Bros. (Figure 2-6) is a relatively simple but classic video game that allows users to see the power of reinforcement learning without adding some of the complexity that we will see in other video game environments later in the book. The player has a number of actions that can be utilized, which are listed at https://github.com/Kautenja/gym-super-mario-bros/blob/master/gym_super_mario_bros/actions.py.

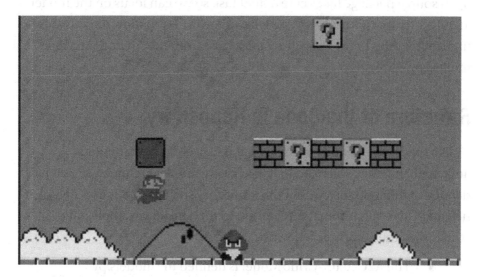

Figure 2-6. Super Mario Bros. Screenshot

The objective of every level is the same: We are trying to avoid all obstacles and enemies so we can touch the flag pole at the end to win the level. The flag pole will always be at the rightmost end of the level, and although there are other bonuses such as mushrooms and brief invincibility that we can gain, those are not the primary goals. For this example, we will not specifically worry about the separate goal of most users, which is to reach the flag, since this will likely be very difficult to train a model for and is only an added bonus.

Installing Environment Package

For this particular environment, users are encouraged to utilize gym-super-mario-bros which can be installed utilizing the following command:

```
pip3 install gym-super-mario-bros
```

Super Mario Bros. is not a standard environment provided in the gym package, so an environment needs to be created. Thankfully, this open source package takes care of that task so we can focus on the model architecture for this problem. We will work with Tensorflow directly this time rather than Keras but will access a class from the "neural_networks/models.py" directory.

Structure of the Code in Repository

Unlike the prior example, from this point forward readers should anticipate that they will need to reference the model architecture as it is defined in different files within the repository such as under the "neural_neworks" and "algorithms" directories. In this specific example, the structure of the code is as follows:

- The A2C Actor-Critic Model is defined in "models.py" as a class.

- "algorithms/actor_critic_utilities" contains the Model and Runner classes. These, including the ActorCriticModel, are all instantiated within the learn_policy() function defined within this file. This is the function in which most of the computation will end up occurring.

These classes and functions are taken from the baselines library released by OpenAI and slightly modified. The reasoning behind this is that rather than working through this manually, it is important for the reader to understand **why** and **how** these models work rather than simply calling them. As such, let us first begin by discussing the model we are using and why.

Model Architecture

For this problem, we will be treating this as an image recognition problem. As such, we will be using a simple LeNet Architecture, which is a type of Convolutional Neural Network architecture. Popular for image recognition, these were first developed by Yann LeCun in the late 1980s. Figure 2-7 shows a typical LeNet Architecture.

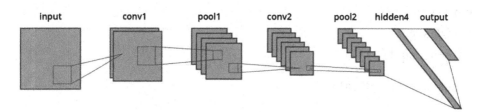

Figure 2-7. *LeNet Architecture*

We will treat each frame as a picture, convolve over this frame to create feature maps, and then continuously reduce the dimensionality of these feature maps until we reach our softmax encoded output vector from which we will randomly choose actions and then eventually train on this batch in the same way we did in the prior vanilla policy gradient example. Readers will now observe the code that details the ActorCriticModel() class that we have created that contains the model architecture and relevant attributes:

```
self.distribution_type = make_pdtype(action_space)
height, weight, channel = environment.shape
environment_shape = (height, weight, channel)
```

```
    inputs_ = tf.placeholder(tf.float32, [None,
    environment_shape], name="input")

    self.distribution_type = make_pdtype(action_space)
    height, weight, channel = environment.shape
    environment_shape = (height, weight, channel)
    inputs_ = tf.placeholder(tf.float32, [None,
    environment_shape], name="input")
    scaled_images = tf.cast(inputs_, tf.float32)/float(255)

    layer1 = tf.layers.batch_normalization(convolution_
    layer(inputs=scaled_images,
filters=32,
kernel_size=8,
strides=4,
gain=np.sqrt(2)))

(code continued later)
```

Before we speak about the implementation of the Actor-Critic Model
to the Super Mario Bros. level, let us briefly discuss what we should do
to preprocess our image data and how it needs to move through the
CNN. Images typically are 256 bits and contain 3 dimensions. What this
means when we process an image into a python matrix is that the matrix
yielded initially should be of dimensions m x n x 3, where m and n are
the length and width, respectively, with each dimension of the matrix
representing a color channel. Specifically, we typically expect the color
channels to represent red, green, and blue. In the instance of Super Mario,
we expect the matrix to appear as in Figure 2-8.

```
array([[[104, 136, 252],
        [104, 136, 252],
        [104, 136, 252],
        ...,
        [104, 136, 252],
        [104, 136, 252],
        [104, 136, 252]],

       [[104, 136, 252],
        [104, 136, 252],
        [104, 136, 252],
        ...,
```

Figure 2-8. *Example of Super Mario Image Matrix (Before Preprocessing)*

To initially reduce complexity of the images, we will grayscale them so that the initially three-dimensional matrix becomes a one-dimensional matrix. The 256 bits each represent a degree of brightness of color with 1 being black and 256 being white. Because python data structures are indexed by 0, 255 is the upper bound, and as such will be what we scale our input images by. Now that we've focused on how we will preprocess our data, that brings us to the first of the convolutional layers that we will be moving through.

Readers will notice that the layers that we make here are utilizing a function that uses a helper function around the convolution layer function native to Tensorflow. In addition to this, we utilize the batch_normalization() on each of the convolutional layers. As stated earlier, the feature maps we will create continue to get smaller. The data that remains is, in theory, the pixels that are the most informative for classification purposes moving forward. Now, we move forward until we flatten all of the feature maps into one array, which we then use to compute $V(s)$. This function's output, as well as other important values, is defined as attributes which we will call during the training of this model.

Moving forward from the ActorCriticModel, let us discuss the Model()
class, whose code is shown as follows:

```
class Model(object):
    def __init__(self, policy_model, observation_space, action_
    space, n_environments,
                n_steps, entropy_coefficient, value_
                coefficient, max_grad_norm):
```

```
(code redacted, please see github)
        train_model = policy_model(session, observation_
        space, action_space, n_environments*n_steps, n_steps,
        reuse=True)
        error_rate = tf.nn.sparse_softmax_cross_entropy_with_
        logits(logits=train_model.logits, labels=actions_)
      mean_squared_error = tf.reduce_mean(advantages_ * error_rate)

        value_loss = tf.reduce_mean(mse(tf.squeeze(train_model.
        value_function) ,rewards_))
        entropy = tf.reduce_mean(train_model.distribution_type.
        entropy())
        loss = mean_squared_error - entropy * entropy_
        coefficient + value_loss * value_coefficient
```

```
(code continued later)
```

In the code, we start with "policy_model()" which is in actuality the
ActorCriticModel() class that we discussed earlier. After this has been
instantiated and passed through this class, we take the error rate from the
individual iteration as it would have occurred within the Model() class.
What readers see immediately should be familiar from standard neural

network training utilizing Tensorflow. Moving forward, let us inspect the Runner() class

```
class Runner(AbstractEnvRunner):
    def __init__(self, environment, model, nsteps, total_
    timesteps, gamma, _lambda):
        super().__init__(environment=environment, model=model,
        n_steps=n_steps)

        self.gamma = gamma
        self._lambda = _lambda
        self.total_timesteps = total_timesteps

    def run(self):
        _observations, _actions, _rewards, _values, _dones =
        [],[],[],[],[]

        for _ in range(self.n_steps):
            actions, values = self.model.step(self.obs, self.
            dones)
            _observations.append(np.copy(self.observations))
            _actions.append(actions)
            _values.append(values)
            _dones.append(self.dones)
            self.observations[:], rewards, self.dones, _ =
            self.environment.step(actions)
            _rewards.append(rewards)
```

(code continued later!)

Readers will observe that we have defined in the previous section of code some variables that we saw in the last example. Specifically, we define gamma which will be utilized as a discount factor. Again, it is significantly easier for gradient descent to work with smaller gradients to optimize weights than it is for the network to work with larger values.

As we go through each of the iterations through the maximum amount of steps we are allowed to take through this environment, we append to the observations, actions, values, rewards, and the Boolean term which determines whether we have failed or are still playing the current episode.

```
(code redacted, please see Github)
delta = _rewards[t] + self.gamma * nextvalues *
nextnonterminal - _values[t]
            _advantages[t] = last_lambda = delta + self.gamma *
self._lambda * nextnonterminal * last_lambda

        _returns = _advantages + _values
        return map(swap_flatten_axes, (_observations, _actions,
        _returns, _values))
```

In the code, we move to the end of the function, where we calculate the delta, or the difference between each individual step with respect to the rewards, lambda, returns, etc. This finally leads us to the "train_model()" function, shown as follows:

```
    model = ActorCriticModel(policy=policy,
            obsevration_space=observation_space,
            action_space=action_space,
            n_environments=n_environments,
n_steps=n+steps,
entropy_coefficient=entropy_coefficient,
value_coefficient=value_coefficient,
max_grad_norm=max_grad_norm)

    model.load("./models/260/model.ckpt")

    runner = Runner(environment,
                    model=model,
                    n_steps=n_steps,
                    n_timesteps=n_timesteps,
```

```
gamma=gamma,
_lambda=_lambda)
```

(code redacted please see github)

As readers have been introduced to these functions, they are now instantiated given the hyperparameters we define at the header of the file as well as within the train_model() function. From this point, the processes that readers see should mirror that of the prior example, with respect to training the model. Now that we have given a proper overview of this example, let us discuss the challenges of trying to train a model like this and results that we observed.

Working with a More Difficult Reinforcement Learning Challenge

The cart pole problem and other classic control problems within RL are relatively easy in that it will not take an inordinate amount of time for whatever method you choose to converge on an optimal solution. For more abstract problems, however, particularly those similar to this example, training times can increase exponentially for the task. For example, there are implementations of A2C and A3C that have been applied to *Sonic the Hedgehog* that still cannot complete a level after 10 hours. Although there are complexities in that example that aren't present here in Super Mario Bros., the same point should be taken to heart. As such, for a problem like this, we are going to need to use a cloud solution. While we will go over AWS and how to use it at a later point, I think it is important for readers to learn other frameworks as well. Because of this, we will work with Google Cloud. As an added bonus, they still give free credits to new users, which will make using this code significantly easier.

Any data scientist or machine learning engineer will reach a point where the solutions they want to make should be productionized and experimented with utilizing cloud resources. AWS and Google Cloud are two solutions that readers should become familiar with not only will come across a point at which it makes sense to start putting code in production. An example of the Google Cloud Dashboard is given as such in Figure 2-9.

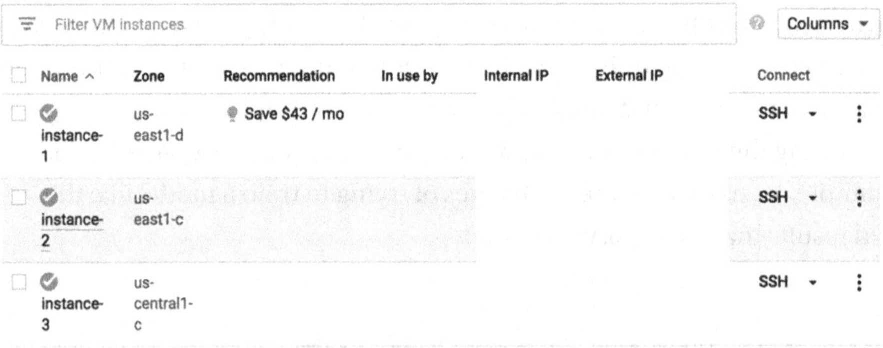

☰ Filter VM instances							⊘ Columns ▾
☐ Name ∧	Zone	Recommendation	In use by	Internal IP	External IP		Connect
☐ ✓ instance-1	us-east1-d	💡 Save $43 / mo					SSH ▾ ⋮
☐ ✓ instance-2	us-east1-c						SSH ▾ ⋮
☐ ✓ instance-3	us-central1-c						SSH ▾ ⋮

Figure 2-9. *Example of Google Cloud Dashboard*

Readers should expect when clicking the SSH icon that they will load a (assumedly here Linux) terminal which will require some standard installation (installing Git, different python packages, etc.). Nothing that the user does here will be terribly different from what they have done on their local machine; however, there will be some syntax differences assuming that you are utilizing Linux.

The important part from this section is to understand that you should be training solutions such as these on Cloud Resources AND NOT on your local machine.

Let us now look at the main function which will actually run the game itself:

```python
def play_super_mario(policy_model=ActorCriticModel,
environment=environment):
    (code redacted, please see github)
        observations = environment.reset()
        score, n_step, done = 0, 0, False

        while done == False:

            actions, values = model.step(observations)
            import pdb; pdb.set_trace()

            for action in actions:

                observations, rewards, done, info =
                environment.step(action)
                score += rewards
                environment.render()
    n_step += 1

            print('Step: %s \nScore: %s '%(n_step, score))
            environment.close()
```

With this last piece of code, we have reviewed all of the necessary classes. The final part that we should discuss here is implementing the training processes smoothly. For this, I recommend that users familiarize themselves with docker.

Dockerizing Reinforcement Learning Experiments

When you are training a reinforcement learning agent, you will likely not want to sit and stare at the agent familiarizing itself with the environment via optimizing its policy and you will most certainly still need your computer in the many hours that you are utilizing to train it. As such, this is why we utilize cloud resources. However, just running your application on a cloud environment *will not* be sufficient. On AWS or Google Cloud, if you do not run the process in the background, the moment at which the connection is lost, either because your computer died, froze, etc., you will lose all of your progress and have to start either from the last checkpoint or from the beginning depending on whether you have modified the code to save along certain checkpoints. As such, it is important that you utilize docker containers.

Docker containers are an interesting solution that allow you to create a virtual environment of the application that you are running from a terminal. Simply stated, you can create a virtual "instance" that quickly spins up your application and runs it from this virtual environment. Another added benefit is that docker includes several commands that can help you by running a process such as this and restarting it in case it stops. In the context of the task we are performing here, we can terminate the process once we have felt we have trained our agent long enough, check the progress of our agent afterward, and then return to training if we deem necessary. First, let us look at an example Docker file.

```
FROM python:3

COPY .git / .git
COPY    init   .py .
COPY repo/ repo
COPY repo2/ repo
COPY repo3/ repo

RUN pip install pandas numpy
```

Figure 2-10. *Example Docker File*

Figure 2-10 is a dummy Docker file where we see three commands that we will review. Specifically, they are "FROM," "COPY," and "RUN." "FROM" is what we define the version of python in which we would like this container to run. Although there are some examples in this book that utilize python2, all should be compatible with python3, and python2 will be not supported past 2020. Moving forward, "COPY" indicates the specific files within a repository that we want to use. Finally, we get to "RUN" where we specifically install the python packages that we need.

It is important to note that you must indicate all of the necessary files, repositories, and python modules in your docker file when you instantiate a new container. If you do not do this, your docker container will not be able to execute the code.

We typically create a container with the following command:

```
"sudo docker -t build . [container name] . "
```

Assuming docker is installed and no files that we are copying are missing, this should create a docker container by the name specified. After this step, users are suggested to run the following command to commence the file.

```
"sudo docker run --dit --restart-unless-stopped python3 -m
path.to.file"
```

Results of the Experiment

This was largely done for illustrative purposes; however, it is useful when working through more difficult reinforcement learning problems to highlight this point – **you must train your agent for a large amount of time.** Unlike some of the more vanilla machine learning examples, and more similar to difficult natural language processing problems that utilize deep learning, training will take a very long time to be effective. In this particular instance, the agent usually runs out of time because it gets stuck on some obstacle like a pipe relatively early on, or it gets unlucky and gets killed relatively quickly by an enemy combatant like a goomba. When the agent is trained for 5 hours, we observe generally that it performs significantly better, most specifically notified by the fact that it is now able to avoid dying, by and large, from any of the enemies in the space. However, it does get caught on obstacles and is not likely to backtrack to find alternative paths forward should it get stuck. The most successful agents were those trained for above 12 hours; however, this solution generally is not finished nor is it necessarily perfect. Much of the success of the agent often seems to be determined by the actions that it takes at critical points, particularly timing jumps properly, and it tends to avoid killing enemies as much as it prefers trying to not fall into the holes in the level. On some occasions, this allows Mario to win; however, what is important to note is that this is one of the more simple levels that the game features.

Conclusion

Readers after this chapter should feel comfortable in applying some basic and one more advanced type of Reinforcement Learning algorithm which are based on episodic and temporal difference methods. The key takeaways from the chapter are the following:

- **Understand the problem type you are tackling** – Similar to most machine learning problems, there are different models to use for different types of data. Are you dealing with a large state space? Is your task episodic? If not, do you realistically want/need to base the learning of the algorithm on more granular steps? Take time to think about these before you approach the solutions.

- **Training RL solutions on difficult problems is time-consuming, so train on cloud resources** – Similar to some advanced NLP problems, readers will observe that local machines are not the place to be training models on. Although it obviously makes sense to be writing most of the code from your local machine, seek to utilize these somewhere else.

With the first type of algorithms now completed, we will move forward to tackling different value-based methods such as Q learning and Deep Q Learning. In the upcoming chapter, we will again take the same precedent of dealing with a more simple problem and then moving to a more complex problem with a considerably larger environment.

CHAPTER 3

Reinforcement Learning Algorithms: Q Learning and Its Variants

With the preliminary discussion on policy gradients and Actor-Critic Models finished, we can now discuss alternative deep learning algorithms that readers might find useful. Specifically, we will discuss Q learning, Deep Q Learning, as well as Deep Deterministic Policy Gradients. Once we have covered these, we will be well versed enough to start dealing with more abstract problems that are more domain specific that will teach the user about how to approach reinforcement learning to different tasks.

Q Learning

Q learning is a part of a family of model-free learning algorithms which learns a policy by looking at all of the possible actions and evaluating each of them. In this algorithm, there are two matrices which we will frequently reference: the Q matrix and the R matrix. The former represents the algorithm's namesake and contains the accumulated knowledge on the environment in which we are implementing a policy. All of the entries

© Taweh Beysolow II 2019
T. Beysolow II, *Applied Reinforcement Learning with Python*,
https://doi.org/10.1007/978-1-4842-5127-0_3

in this matrix are initialized at 0 and the goal is to maximize the reward yielded. Upon each step in the environment, the Q matrix is updated. The R matrix is the environment where each row represents a state and the columns represent the awards for moving to another state. The structure of this matrix is similar to a correlation matrix, where each row and column index mirror one another. We have visualizations of both a Q and an R matrix in Figures 3-1 and 3-2.

$$Q = \begin{array}{c} \\ 0 \\ 1 \\ 2 \\ 3 \\ 4 \\ 5 \end{array} \begin{array}{cccccc} 0 & 1 & 2 & 3 & 4 & 5 \\ \left[\begin{array}{cccccc} 0 & 0 & 0 & 0 & 0 & 0 \\ 0 & 0 & 0 & 0 & 0 & 100 \\ 0 & 0 & 0 & 0 & 0 & 0 \\ 0 & 80 & 0 & 0 & 0 & 0 \\ 0 & 0 & 0 & 0 & 0 & 0 \\ 0 & 0 & 0 & 0 & 0 & 0 \end{array}\right] \end{array}$$

Figure 3-1. *Visualization of Q Table*

Action

$$R = \begin{array}{c} \text{State} \\ 0 \\ 1 \\ 2 \\ 3 \\ 4 \\ 5 \end{array} \begin{array}{cccccc} 0 & 1 & 2 & 3 & 4 & 5 \\ \left[\begin{array}{cccccc} -1 & -1 & -1 & -1 & 0 & -1 \\ -1 & -1 & -1 & 0 & -1 & 100 \\ -1 & -1 & -1 & 0 & -1 & -1 \\ -1 & 0 & 0 & -1 & 0 & -1 \\ 0 & -1 & -1 & 0 & -1 & 100 \\ -1 & 0 & -1 & -1 & 0 & 100 \end{array}\right] \end{array}$$

Figure 3-2. *Visualization of R Table*

The agent can see the R table with respect to the immediate actions it can take within it, but cannot see anything else. Because of this limitation, this is precisely where the Q table becomes important. The Q table as mentioned earlier contains all of the accumulated information about the environment that it populates over a given period. In some sense, we can think of the Q table as the map and the R table as the world. Specifically how the Q table is updated is given by the following:

$$Q(s_t, a_t) := Q(s_t, a_t) + \alpha \left[\left(r(s_t, a_t) + \gamma . \max \{ Q(s_{t+1}, a_{t+1}) \} \right) - Q(s_t, a_t) \right]$$

where $Q(s_t, a_t)$ = the cell entry, α = learning rate, γ = discount factor, $\max\{Q(s_{t+1}, a_{t+1})\}$) = maximum Q table value.

Temporal Difference (TD) Learning

In the introduction chapter, we briefly touched upon the topic of Markov decision process. To reiterate more specifically, MDPs refer to events that are partially random but also are dependent upon or in control of a decision maker. We define a MDP as the following 4-tuple:

$$\left(S, A, P_a, R_a \right)$$

where S = set representing the states, A = set representing the allowable actions, P_a = probability that action a in state s at time t results in state s' at time $t + 1$, R_a= immediate reward received after transitioning from state s to state s' due to action a.

As a reminder, Figure 3-3 is an example of the Markov decision-making process.

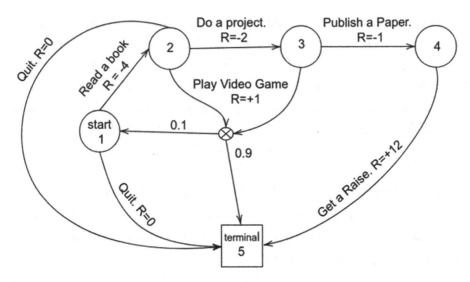

Figure 3-3. *Markov Decision-Making Process*

As we have stated earlier, most of reinforcement learning revolves around states from which we can perform actions that yield a reward as well. The goal we are trying to reach is choosing the optimal policy for the decision maker that maximizes the reward yielded. We briefly brought up temporal difference learning in the introduction, but now is an appropriate time to discuss this at length.

TD learning is broadly described as a method to predict a quantity that depends on the future values of a specific signal. It refers to the "temporal differences" in predictions over varying timesteps. TD learning is designed such that the prediction at a current timestep is updated to so that the following prediction for the next timestep is correct. Q learning itself is an example of TD learning. One way in which we can solve a TD learning problem, specifically as it manifests here, is the epsilon-greedy algorithm.

Epsilon-Greedy Algorithm

Eventually, after a large amount of iterations, the Q table is good enough to be utilized directly by an agent. To get to this point, we want the Q learning algorithm to utilize the information in the table less than it explores. This is what at large is described as the exploration-exploitation trade-off, and it is controlled by the epsilon parameter. The key here is that the first possible path that might be utilized to reach a solution is not guaranteed to be the best path. With this being stated, it is unlikely that it will always be the case that if we keep searching, we will find a better solution than the current one, and therefore we abstain from solving the problem. To mitigate this issue, it is recommended to use the epsilon-greedy algorithm.

Epsilon-greedy algorithm is within the family of the multi-armed bandit problem. This is described as a problem where we must choose between a variety of options with the end goal of maximizing a reward. The classic example to illustrate this problem is to imagine a casino where we have four machines, each with different unknown reward probabilities. We describe a Bernoulli multi-armed bandit as a set actions and rewards represented respectively in the tuple <A, R> where there are K machines with reward probabilities $\{\theta_1, ..., \theta_K\}$. Each action corresponds to an interaction with a respective slot machine, and rewards are stochastic in that they will return with a probability of $Q(a_t)$ or 0 otherwise. The expected reward is represented as the following equation:

$$Q(a_k) = \mathbb{E}[r_k | a_k] = \theta_k, k \in \{1, ..., k\}$$

And our goal is to maximize the cumulative reward by choosing the optimal actions, where the optimal reward probability and loss functions are given respectively by the following equations:

$$\theta^* = Q(a^*) = \max_{a \in A} Q(a) = \max_{1 \le i \le K} \theta_i$$

$$L_T = \mathbb{E}\left[\sum_{t=1}^{T}\left(\theta^* - Q(a_t)\right)\right]$$

Although there are multiple ways to solve the multi-armed bandit problem, we will focus here on the   strategy. This is an algorithm that estimates the quality of the action via the following equation:

$$\hat{Q}_t(a) = \frac{1}{N_t(a)}\sum_{\tau=1}^{t} r_\tau \, \mathbb{1}[a_\tau = a]$$

where $N_t(a)$ = number of times action a has been taken, $\mathbb{1}$ = binary indicator function.

If ϵ is small, then we will explore our immediate environment. However, otherwise, we will utilize the best possible action that we know at this moment. To illustrate the entirety of the Q learning algorithm, we will learn to play a game called "Frozen Lake."

Frozen Lake Solved with Q Learning

Frozen Lake is a game provided in Gym in which the player is trying to train an agent to walk across a lake from a starting point to another end point on the lake. However, not all of the patches of ice are frozen, in which stepping on this would cause us to lose the game. We do not receive any rewards except for reaching the goal. Readers can imagine the environment looking like the following image (Figure 3-4).

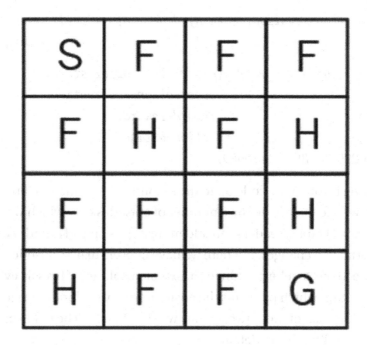

Figure 3-4. *Frozen Lake Environment*

Similar to most of the other files we have written, we started by defining the parameters we can use later as well as the environment. The two main functions populate_q_matrix() and play_frozen_lake() contain within them many of the helper functions defined earlier. Let's start first by walking through the function that populates the Q matrix.

```
def populate_q_table(render=False, n_episodes=n_episodes):
(documentation redacted, please see github)
    for episode in range(n_episodes):
        prior_state = environment.reset()
        _ = 0
        while _ < max_steps:
            if render == True: environment.render()
            action = exploit_explore(prior_state)
```

```
observation, reward, done, info = environment.
                                      step(action)

update_q_matrix(prior_state=prior_state,
                observation=observation,
                reward=reward,
                action=action)
(CODE TO BE CONTINUED)
```

Walking through the code up to the second helper function, update_q_matrix(), we see that we define a number of episodes over which we will populate the Q table. Readers can add more or less episodes and see how the performance changes, but here we have chosen 10,000 episodes. We now come to our first helper function, exploit_explore(). This self-evidently is the algorithm which performs the epsilon-greedy exploration algorithm to determine what of those two actions we should take. The following function describes this in detail.

```
def exploit_explore(prior_state, epsilon=epsilon):
(documentation redacted, please read github)
    if np.random.uniform(0, 1) < epsilon:
        return environment.action_space.sample()
    else:
        return np.argmax(Q_matrix[prior_state, :])
```

As readers can see, we only explore with a random action in the instance that the value we randomly pull from the uniform distribution is 0. Otherwise, we choose the best possible action we are aware of given that state. Moving forward in the body of the larger function, continue as we have in prior examples by having the agent perform an action within the environment. This yields the difference; however, now we must update the Q matrix.

```
def update_q_matrix(prior_state, observation , reward, action):
prediction = Q_matrix[prior_state, action]
    actual_label = reward + gamma * np.max(Q_
    matrix[observation, :])
    Q_matrix[prior_state, action] = Q_matrix[prior_state,
    action] + learning_rate*(actual_label - prediction)
```

Per the earlier equation, we update the Q matrix's entry where each column represents an action to be taken and each row represents a different state. We continue this process within each episode until we either hit the maximum number of steps we are allowed to take or we fall through the ice. Once we have reached the maximum number of episodes, we are ready to play the game using our Q table. Readers should observe the game when it is running in the terminal to appear as in Figure 3-5.

Figure 3-5. *Frozen Lake Game*

The terminal will output messages when you win or lose during a given episode. We generally observe over multiple experiments using the parameters provided that the agent will generally win two to three times over 10 episodes and will reach a solution in approximately 20–30 steps.

The main advantage to Q learning to some degree is that it does not require a model and that the algorithm is fairly transparent. It is easy to explain why the agent at a given state in time will choose an action. With that being said, the main drawback to this is that the experience necessary to gain knowledge of what to do at a given state is very computationally

expensive when we are dealing with very large environments if we are
to sufficiently fill the Q matrix with information. While this frozen lake
example is fairly constrained, environments such as more complex video
games will likely take an exceptionally long time to get a good Q table.
To overcome this limitation, Deep Q Learning was designed.

Deep Q Learning

Deep Q Learning is fairly straightforward coming from Q learning In
that the only real difference between the two methods is that DQL
approximates the values in the Q table rather than trying to populate them
manually. Precisely how this is done is the linkage between the epsilon-
greedy search (or an alternative algorithm) and the outcome of the actions.
The epsilon-greedy search algorithm solves for how do we decide whether
to exploit or explore and we in turn update the Q matrix based on the
value of the actions at that state. In this sense, we can see that we want to
minimize the loss between reaching our goal and the action we take. In
this sense, we now have something to utilize gradient descent on, which is
represented as the following equation:

$$\mathcal{L}_i\left(\theta_i\right) = \mathbb{E}_{a \sim \mu}\left[\left(y_i - Q\left(s, a; \theta_i\right)\right)^2\right],$$

$$y_i := \mathbb{E}_{a' \sim \mu}[r + \gamma \max_{a'} Q\left(s', a'; \theta_{i-1}\right) | S_t = s, A_t = a]$$

where μ = behavior policy, θ = neural network parameters.

Both the target label and the Q matrix are predicted by two separate
neural networks. The target network shares the weights and biases of the
Q network, but they are updated after the Q network. Moving forward,
however, let us discuss the importance of experience replay and how
we utilize it here. Neural networks will overwrite the weights if we
introduce completely new data in the context of reinforcement learning.

As such, this is why often there are different models that are trained for different purposes. Experience replay is how we make usage of observed experiences by storing them and then this helps to reduce the correlation we might observe between experiences. Practically speaking, we save in memory the tuple we introduced in the beginning of the chapter. During training, we will calculate the target label with the tuple and then apply gradient descent such that we have weights and biases that will generalize well on the entire environment. Moving forward, however, let us now try to work through a problem using Deep Q Learning and see how the complexity of our problem has changed significantly.

Playing Doom with Deep Q Learning

One of the classic examples for utilizing DQL is the original Doom video game, shown in Figure 3-6, whose environment is also an excellent one in which to test various machine learning algorithms. Doom is a first person shooter in which the player must navigate a three-dimensional environment in which they are fighting against enemy combatants. Because this is an older 3D game, the player moves around in the environment in the same way many of our theoretical agents do in a Q matrix. This will be the first continuous control problem in which we apply Reinforcement Learning.

Figure 3-6. An Example of a Level Within Doom

Simply stated, we distinguish continuous control systems from discrete control by systems in which the variables and parameters would be continuous in the former and discrete in the latter. An example of a continuous process in the context of reinforcement learning would be driving a car or teaching a robot to walk. An example of discrete control processes would be the first problem we dealt with, the cart pole, as well as other problems within the "classic control" problems such as swinging a pendulum. Although there are plenty of discrete tasks worth analyzing for the sake of understanding the algorithms, many tasks that would be useful to implement with reinforcement learning are continuous. This along with the massive size of the state space makes this an excellent candidate for Deep Q Learning. We will attack this problem by looking at the difference in a simple level vs. a more difficult level and seeing the difference in algorithm performance.

Specific to the game itself, the goal is fairly straightforward. We must complete the level without dying which ostensibly requires killing enemy combatants along our way to the end of the level. Most of the enemies will retaliate preemptively, so the algorithm will be mainly focused upon training on how to react based on this. Broadly speaking, the two major processes we will be performing via this algorithm are (1) sampling the environment and storing the experiences in the MDP tuple and (2) selecting some of these to utilize as batch training examples. Let us begin by first discussing how we will preprocess our data for this model in addition to what type of model architecture we will utilize.

```
class DeepQNetwork():

    def __init__(self, n_units, n_classes, n_filters, stride,
    kernel, state_size, action_size, learning_rate):
    (code redacted, please see github)
        self.input_matrix = tf.placeholder(tf.float32, [None,
        *state_size])
        self.actions = tf.placeholder(tf.float32, [None])
        self.target_Q = tf.placeholder(tf.float32, [None,
        *state_size])

        self.network1 = convolution_layer(inputs=self.input_matrix,
                                    filters=self.n_filters,
                                    kernel_size=self.kernel,
                                    strides=self.stride,
                                    activation='elu')
(code redacted please see github)
```

Similar to prior Tensorflow graphs that we have defined as graphs, we will begin by defining a couple of particular attributes. These will be utilized later in the "play_doom()" function in doom_example.py, but we will address those later. Moving forward, we can see that similar to the example we utilized in Super Mario Bros, we will want to use a LeNet Architecture, except in this instance, we will be utilizing a layer that accepts four dimensions since we are attacking the frames. We similarly eventually flatten the feature maps into an array which we then will output via a fully connected softmax layer. From this softmax layer, we will sample our actions during training. Figure 3-7 shows an example of the model architecture we will be utilizing for our Deep Q Network.

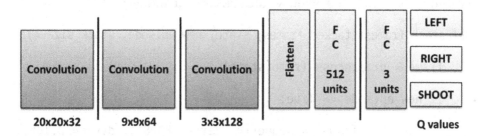

Figure 3-7. *Example Architecture for Deep Q Network*

Moving backward to discussing the input data, in the prior example we did not stack the frames and instead passed the current and prior states as they were, being reformatted matrices of the input data. The reasoning behind why this is important, particularly in a three-dimensional environment is because it gives the Deep Q Network an understanding of the motion that the agent is inducing. This method was proposed by Deep Mind. We preprocess and stack the frames via the following function:

```
def preprocess_frame(frame):
    cropped_frame = frame[30:-10,30:-30]
    normalized_frame = cropped_frame/float(255)
    preprocessed_frame = transform.resize(normalized_frame,
    [84,84])
    return preprocessed_frame
```

We first begin by utilizing a grayscaled image, which is given to us in this form by the vizdoom library thankfully. In the event that this was not grayscale, users should utilize a library such as **OpenCV** to perform this preprocessing. Moving forward, we will scale the pixel values again by 255 as we did in the Super Mario example and for the same reasoning. One minor difference however, is that we will be cropping out the top of the frame in this initial example, since the ceiling in Doom is just for atmospheric purposes and doesn't contain anything worth evaluating. We utilize the preceding function here when we are stacking the frames:

```
def stack_frames(stacked_frames, state, new_episode, stack_size=4):

    frame = preprocess_frame(state)

    if new_episode == True:

        stacked_frames = deque([np.zeros((84,84), dtype=np.int)
        for i in range(stack_size)], maxlen=4)
        for i in range(4):
            stacked_frames.append(frame)

        stacked_state = np.stack(stacked_frames, axis=2)

    else:

        stacked_frames.append(frame)
        stacked_state = np.stack(stacked_frames, axis=2)

    return stacked_state, stacked_frames
```

The important takeaway from this function, separate from the functions that transform the frames into four stacks, is how precisely this happens. When this function is called for the first time, we take the first four frames. Moving forward, we append the newest frame while deleting the last, such that this process should represent a first in last out (FILO) process. Something to keep in mind, however, is that this process isn't very realistic in the sense that humans would not see multiple frames staggered, but rather would see them all at once. In addition to this, this makes training significantly more difficult because of the memory that is used storing these stacked images. Users should keep this in mind when we are working through different examples in the coming chapters. Moving forward, we will be utilizing a slightly more elaborate greedy epsilon strategy, in which we will also be utilizing a decay rate as shown in the following function:

```
def exploit_explore(session, model, explore_start, explore_
stop, decay_rate, decay_step, state, actions):
    exp_exp_tradeoff = np.random.rand()
    explore_probability = explore_stop + (explore_start -
    explore_stop) * np.exp(-decay_rate * decay_step)

    if (explore_probability > exp_exp_tradeoff):
        action = random.choice(possible_actions)
    else:
        Qs = session.run(model.output, feed_dict = {model.
        input_matrix: state.reshape((1, * state.shape))})
        choice = np.argmax(Qs)
        action = possible_actions[int(choice)]
```

The idea behind this is greedy epsilon strategy is essentially the same as we saw in the original Q learning example, except that the decay is exponential in that it becomes increasingly likely that we will explore less over time forcing the algorithm to utilize its accumulated knowledge. Now with the helper functions explained, let us now walk through the function that will actually be utilized to train the model. Without further ado, let us observe the results from training the model on this level. We will then move to a different level and see how the model performs on.

Simple Doom Level

In this scenario, the player is in a simple environment in which they can move left, right, and/or shoot at the enemy combatant. This enemy combatant will not shoot back and simply moves occasionally to the left or the right. Readers when running the code should expect an output and screenplay to look as shown in Figures 3-8 and 3-9.

```
Episode: 3 Total reward: 94.0 Explore P: 0.9701
Episode: 4 Total reward: 27.0 Explore P: 0.9644
Episode: 13 Total reward: 76.0 Explore P: 0.8893
Episode: 14 Total reward: 91.0 Explore P: 0.8884
Episode: 17 Total reward: 95.0 Explore P: 0.8705
Episode: 20 Total reward: 27.0 Explore P: 0.8485
```

Figure 3-8. *Screenshot of Training Mode*

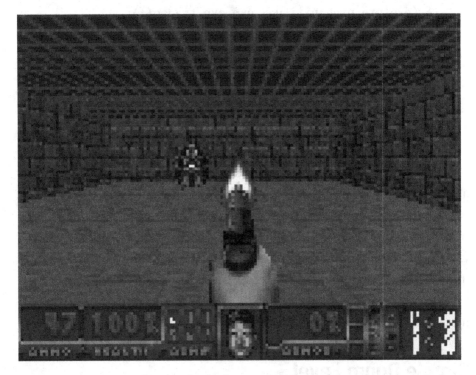

Figure 3-9. *Example of Simple Doom Environment*

Training and Performance

Figure 3-10 shows the results from training the Q matrix over various episodes as well as the out-of-sample results.

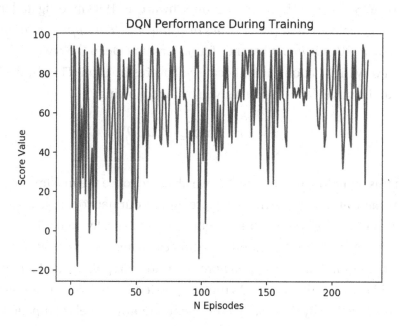

Figure 3-10. *Deep Q Network Scores During Training*

Readers should be aware that tasks like these, as we have spoken about due to the preprocessing and computation being utilized, are considerably memory intensive. In addition to this, there are times where the neural network does not learn appropriately the right course of action to take as it gets stuck in local optima. Although the parameters listed have in general yielded out-of-sample solutions that are acceptable, there were also times where this neural network ***did not*** perform well. This is one of the limitations.

Limitations of Deep Q Learning

Deep Q Learning, as we have shown earlier, is not without its faults. Separate from this example though, where do most of these inefficiencies tend to lie? Sebastian Thrun and Anton Schwartz in 1993 investigated this more specifically in their paper *Issues in Using Function Approximation for Reinforcement Learning*. What they found was that Deep Q Networks often learned very high action values because of overestimation. This, by design, is due to the target label formula given by the following:

$$y_i := \mathbb{E}_{a' \sim \pi}\left[r + \gamma \max_{a'} Q(s', a'; \theta_{i-1}) \right]$$

In this equation, we can see that we always choose the maximum known value at that time, which can preference our network to learn these values at stages where they might be unrealistically high. This is specifically how function approximation can cause overestimation. Overestimation, as it can happen here, leads to poor policies and tends to induce bias within the model. As this manifested in the Doom example, this is exemplified by the fact that the agent oftentimes feels compelled to shoot regardless of its position relative to the enemy. How precisely can this be fixed?

Double Q Learning and Double Deep Q Networks

As highlighted before in the prior equation, the max operator uses the same values to select and evaluate an action given the state of the environment. Precisely when we separate this into two separate processes (selection and evaluation) do we get Double Q Learning. Double Q Learning utilizes two value functions and each of which have two respective weight sets. One of the weight sets is utilized for determining the greedy-epsilon exploit or explore trade-off problem and the other for determining the value of a given action. We then rewrite the target approximation as the following:

$$Y_t^Q = R_{t+1} + \gamma Q\left(S_{t+1}, \, \arg\max_a Q\left(S_{t+1}, a; \theta_t\right); \theta_t\right)$$

With this now explained, we can discuss Double Q Networks and how they are being utilized to overcome the shortcomings of Deep Q Networks. Rather than add additional models, we instead utilize the target network to estimate the value while utilizing the online network to evaluate the explore-exploit decision-making process. The target function for the double Q network is the following:

$$Y_t^{DoubleQN} \equiv R_{t+1} + \gamma Q\left(S_{t+1}, \arg\max_a Q\left(S_{t+1}, a; \theta_t\right), \theta_t^-\right)$$

Conclusion

With both examples of Q learning and Deep Q Learning finished, we advise the reader to try applying these algorithms in a variety of contexts. Where necessary, they can change parameters and fork/change existing code and models. Regardless, what I would suggest to readers to keep in mind moving forward is the following:

- **Q learning is straightforward and easy to explain –**
  The benefit to this algorithm is that it is easy to understand why the Q values are inputted as such. For tasks where implementing algorithms requires transparency, it is not unwise to consider something like this for where it will do.

- **Q learning has limitations on large state spaces!** – While the prior comment holds for simple problems, it is important to realize in instances like the Doom example and more complex environments, Vanilla Q Learning will take an exhaustive amount of time to get through.

- **Deep Q Learning still can fall in local optima!** – Like other reinforcement learning algorithms, DQN can still find locally optimal policies but not the globally optimal policy. Finding this global optimum can be exhaustive from a training standpoint.

- **Try implementing Double Q Learning and Double Deep Q Networks!** – The limitations of Q learning and DQNs have been overcome by increasingly more advanced techniques and at a rapid pace. This starting point should allow you to try implementing state-of-the-art algorithms from scratch.

With these examples finished, let's move on to some other reinforcement learning algorithms that we have not covered yet and discuss these in depth.

CHAPTER 4

Market Making via Reinforcement Learning

Separate from just attacking some of the standard problems in reinforcement learning as they are found in many books as an example, it's good to look at fields where the answers are either not as objective nor completely solved. One of the best examples of this in finance, specifically for reinforcement learning, is market making. We will discuss the discipline itself, present some baseline method that isn't based on machine learning, and then test several reinforcement learning–based methods.

What Is Market Making?

In financial markets, there is constantly a need for liquidity among people that utilize exchanges. It is likely impossible that at any one given moment that every person trying to sell an asset's orders match precisely with the people who want to buy. As such, market makers play a vital role in facilitating the execution of orders from people who typically want to take

© Taweh Beysolow II 2019
T. Beysolow II, *Applied Reinforcement Learning with Python*,
https://doi.org/10.1007/978-1-4842-5127-0_4

a position in a financial instrument (long or short) for a varying duration of time lengths. Typically, market making is described as one of the few ways that people in financial markets can consistently make money in financial markets as opposed to betting models which take riskier bets but ones conditionally with higher payoffs. Let's now try and understand what the data we're working with is and what we can expect. Figure 4-1 is a sample image of an order book with associated orders.

Orderbook (XBTUSD) ⚙ ↗

Price	Size	Total
11169.0	10,412	206,032
11168.0	47,329	195,620
11167.5	57,430	148,291
11167.0	9,999	90,861
11164.5	100	80,862
11164.0	240	80,762
11163.5	2,000	80,522
11163.0	32,370	78,522
11162.5	2,414	46,152
11162.0	43,738	43,738

11162.0 ↑
ⓘ 11129.25 / 11129.79 | □□□□□

11161.5	161,603	161,603
11160.5	40,029	201,632
11160.0	388	202,020
11159.5	737	202,757
11159.0	8,400	211,157
11158.0	10,636	221,793
11157.5	21,100	242,893
11157.0	5,791	248,684
11156.5	38,563	287,247
11156.0	9,800	297,047

Figure 4-1. *Example Order Book*

Figure 4-1 is an example of orders that are sitting on both sides of the order book, representing the bid as well as the ask. When someone sends an order to an exchange and uses a limit order, the quantity they are trying to sell sits on the order book until the order is filled. While the fill algorithms exclusive to the exchange can vary from one to another, they usually seek to fill orders in which they are received such that the most recent order is the last order to be filled. The benefit of utilizing limit orders is that they can significantly reduce what is known as "market impact." To state it simply, whenever someone wants to buy large amounts of something, it signals to the rest of the market that there is significant demand. This means that we can affect our own ability to get the best possible price and fill our own orders. Because of this, traders often scatter their limit orders as to obscure their intentions as best as possible.

To give a more concrete example of market making, let us imagine that we are some financial exchange that has a multitude of customers that typically want to exchange every large order. However, not all of these orders are evenly distributed such that every person who wants to buy has another large customer who wants to sell. We therefore decide to incentivize market makers, typically by offering very preferential fee rates, to provide liquidity such that the orders of these large customers can be facilitated. The better that an exchange is at attracting market makers such that they bring more liquidity, typically the better the exchange is for people who want to trade, particularly institutional buyers.

The basic idea of market making is that someone is generally willing to buy and/or sell an instrument at any given price, such that over time their strategy produces returns for them. The main attractive aspect of market making is that once a successful strategy has been identified that is scalable, it is typically valid for significantly longer periods of time than traditional directional models that hedge funds and other trading desks might take. In addition to this, the risk associated with market making is lower. With this being said, market making's primary difficulty in a practical sense is that depending on the market, it can require a large amount of capital to facilitate making a market. With that being stated, however, we are going to utilize reinforcement learning to try and develop a more intuitive way of developing a strategy rather than trying to perform more traditional quantitative finance research.

Trading Gym

Similar to the OpenAI gym, and the derivatives of that package that we have utilized to play various video games such as *Super Mario Bros.* and *Doom*, readers here will be utilizing Trading Gym. It is an open source project whose goal is to make applying reinforcement learning algorithms in the context of trading easy. In Figure 4-2, you can see the plot that should typically display itself when the environment is rendering.

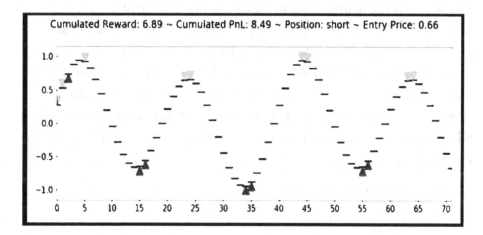

Figure 4-2. *Trading Gym Visualization*

In this environment, readers will typically have three options available to them:

1. Buy the instrument

2. Sell the instrument

3. Hold a current position

Trading Gym typically allows you to work with one (or more) products/ financial instruments where the format of the data is the (bid_product1, ask_product1, bid_product2, ask_product2). We define the *bid* as the best possible price at which an individual can buy a product and the *ask* as the best possible price at which it can be sold. We will walk through with the reader how to import their own order book data to the environment, but prior to that, let us first discuss the problem we are trying to solve and look at a more deterministic method of solving the problem.

Why Reinforcement Learning for This Problem?

Although it is not readily apparent from trading gym, all of market making requires the use of limit orders to be effective. The downside to market orders, because the liquidity needed to fill an order is almost always guaranteed (below certain allocations), is that exchanges typically charge a sizeable fee. Because of this, the only way to utilize a market making strategy is to place orders on the limit order book and allow for them to be filled. With that being stated, this then introduces several problems such as the following:

1.   What price should I buy?

2.   What price should I sell?

3.   What price should I hold?

All of these questions are not easily answered within the context of machine learning. Specifically, the space that we are acting in is continuous. As we stated earlier, the market is continuously changing and our actions on the market itself can make it more difficult to fill, or not fill, our orders. As such, a vanilla machine learning approach doesn't take these environment factors into consideration unless we included them as features. Even then, it would be difficult to try and encode some of these aspects unless we have done a significant amount of research on the market beforehand. Secondarily, most machine learning methods would like be invalid, as this is a time series task. The only appropriate method would be a recurrent neural network (RNN), and particularly because of the granularity of this task, we would have to predict a considerable number of sequences ahead. This would result in a model where we held positions for considerably longer on average than we would like to in market making context. We want agility and flexibility, whereas using a machine learning approach would likely force us to hold positions for predetermined periods of time, rather than when it was most advantageous for us to exit positions based on the market context. All of these reasons justify a reinforcement learning–based approach. Let's move to describing the code and how we can create a reasonable example for us to move on. What follows is an example of the code that will execute the function:

```
memory = Memory(max_size=memory_size)

environment = SpreadTrading(spread_coefficients=[1],
                            data_generator=generator,
                            trading_fee=trading_fee,
                            time_fee=time_fee,

history_length=history_length)

state_size = len(environment.reset())
```

Before we move further, there are a few important attributes that we define for the SpreadTrading() class that we should walk through. Some of these are fairly straightforward as in that all transactions in financial markets cost money to enact on the average exchange, so we must set a fee. In the first example we are utilizing, the exchange data will be synthesized, and the second example will use real order book data. We will charge a nominal fee that does not correspond to any particular exchange.

We set time_fee to 0 as there should be no cost. Most importantly, however, we should discuss the DataGenerator class and what it does.

Synthesizing Order Book Data with Trading Gym

When working with trading gym, we have the option of either directly working with order book data or synthesizing our own. To start, we will be working with the WavySignal function, shown as follows:

```
class WavySignal(DataGenerator):
    def _generator(period_1, period_2, epsilon, ba_spread=0):
        i = 0
        while True:
            i += 1
            bid_price = (1 - epsilon) * np.sin(2 * i * np.pi /
            period_1) + \
                epsilon * np.sin(2 * i * np.pi / period_2)
            yield bid_price, bid_price + ba_spread
```

For those who are unfamiliar with generator functions, they are typically used for instances in which we need to iterate through large amounts of data which we have predetermined where it should be read from; however, it would be too large to store this data in memory given the nature of the application we are seeking. Instead, the objects are stored. Moving forward, however, this generator will generate fake data based on the preceding logic. With our generator working, we run the file using the following command:

```
"pythonw -m chapter4.market_making_example"
```

We should observe an output similar to that in Figure 4-3.

```
('Episode: 0', 'Total reward: -12.6', 'Loss: 2.69732347569e-10', 'Explore P: 0.9901')
('Episode: 1', 'Total reward: -13.755527185', 'Loss: 0.000434227811638', 'Explore P: 0.9804')
('Episode: 2', 'Total reward: -13.8', 'Loss: 0.00019776969566', 'Explore P: 0.9707')
('Episode: 3', 'Total reward: -13.0', 'Loss: 3.77897376893e-05', 'Explore P: 0.9612')
('Episode: 4', 'Total reward: -11.2', 'Loss: 0.000217975015403', 'Explore P: 0.9517')
```

Figure 4-3. *Output from WavySignal Data Generator*

On this particular example, we are utilizing a Deep Q Network to solve this problem. As we can see, the DQN prefers to exploit the environment more over time rather than emphasizing exploration. This, in addition to accrued knowledge, is leading us to achieve higher scores than we were at earlier episodes. Because this is synthesized data, there is no necessary reason to continue analyzing this problem. This is helpful for when the focus we place is training and selecting algorithms. However, in a real-world context, we obviously want to solve problems in order to figure out what would be a solution we could deploy in a real-life scenario.

Generating Order Book Data with Trading Gym

In this environment, we have two choices: (1) use fake data or (2) use real market data. Besides familiarizing yourself with how the environment works, I don't think fake data has much utility. As such, we're going to start utilizing real data. This brings us to the CSVStreamer() class, which is shown as follows:

```
class CSVStreamer(DataGenerator):
def _generator(filename, header=False):
        with open(filename, "r") as csvfile:
            reader = csv.reader(csvfile)
            if header:
```

```
        next(reader, None)
    for row in reader:
        #assert len(row) % 2 == 0
        yield np.array(row, dtype=np.float)
```

(code redacted, please see tgym github!)

The CSVStreamer class essentially can be summarized by the _generator() function, which we showed in the code previously. It simply looks through each of the rows in the file assuming the first column is the bid and second is the ask. Readers can download data from LOBSTER that allows them to get different order book data or seek to buy this data from a provider such as Bloomberg. This repository can be accessed through the following URL: https://lobsterdata.com/.

This is obviously considerably expensive, so it should be reserved for people who have large research budgets and/or work at an institution who already has a Bloomberg terminal available. The "generator" variable we will be using in this example is the CSVStreamer loading the order book data that is included in this repository. Moving forward, let us begin by inspecting the function that will be performing most of the computation in this example:

```
def train_model(model, environment):
(code redacted, please see github)
            while step < max_steps:

                step += 1; decay_step += 1

                action, explore_probability = exploit_explore(...)
                state, reward, done, info = environment.step(action)
```

Similar to the *Doom* example we showed in the prior chapter, most of the code ends up being homogenous and similar. We are going to iterate over the environment in the same fashion as earlier, except here, we will be focusing on comparing the performance of multiple approaches and evaluating which one we should use.

Experimental Design

While it is rarely public precisely what market makers use as their algorithms, generally speaking we want to utilize a simple set of rules. The following algorithms will form our control group and a basic understanding of why a rules-based system is superior to that of a randomly generated set of choices. As with other experiments, the purpose of the control group will allow us to compare the results of our models against it to see if we have exceeded the benchmark set by the control group. This new set of approaches will form the experimental group. We will evaluate the success of the algorithms based on the following criteria:

- The overall reward

- The average reward over the entirety of the experiment

Without further ado, let us discuss how we arrive at the control group/ baseline algorithm. The following lists the requirements for our two strategies:

Strategy 1 (Experiment group)

- Randomly select all options.

Strategy 2 (Control group)

- Randomly select buy, hold, sell.

- If the position is long, sell the asset.

- If the position is short, buy the asset.

- If we are holding a cash position, randomly select an option.

The code for both strategies will be executed by the baseline_model() function, which we show as follows:

```
def baseline_model(n_actions, info, random=True):

    if random == True:
        action = np.random.choice(range(n_actions),
        p=np.repeat(1/float(n_actions), 3))
        action = possible_actions[action]

    else:

        if len(info) == 0:
            action = np.random.choice(range(n_actions),
            p=np.repeat(1/float(n_actions), 3))
            action = possible_actions[action]

        elif info['action'] == 'sell':
            action = buy

        else:
            action = sell

    return action
```

Readers should be familiar by now with the "info" dictionary which displays the information from the environment where there is something relevant. In Trading Gym, the info dictionary displays the most recent action. In the event that we are holding cash, the dictionary will be empty. In the event that we are having a position open, it will read under the "action" key, "buy" or "sell," and sometimes the most recent profit from the last action taken in the event that we were not holding cash. For the preceding experiment, we will be repeating 100 individual trades over 1000 trials. In the end after we have trained our model, we will repeat this same scheme and compare the results. The following results we yielded from our experiment utilizing both of the respective strategies:

- **Strategy 1 average reward** – 30,890

- **Strategy 2 average reward** – 62,777

We have the following distribution and data associated with these experiments (Figures 4-4 and 4-5).

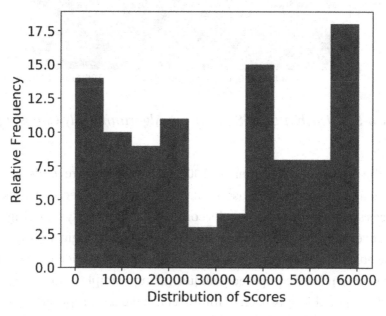

Figure 4-4. *Distribution of Scores from Randomly Choosing Actions*

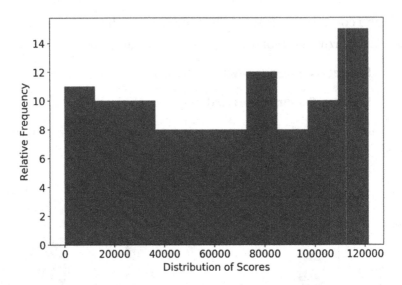

Figure 4-5. *Distribution of Scores from Algorithmically Choosing Answers*

As the preceding experiment of 1000 trials shows, the rewards we choose when there is some reasonable logic behind our decision-making produces significantly better results compared to randomly choosing actions over the entirety of these trials. As such, by that logic, we should then be able to further increase our yields if we find a model that optimally chooses these results compared with just taking a simple heuristic as we did earlier. With this approach in mind, let us take our proposed solutions.

RL Approach 1: Policy Gradients

While vanilla policy gradients do have their shortcomings, there are a relatively restricted amount of decisions that would allow us to easily iterate through the choices. The negative to this space is that we might not be capturing the continuous element of our state space. With this being stated, we have one immediate problem that we should address, which is the loss function. When we first utilized policy gradients, we only had two classes and were operating in a discrete sample space. As such, we were able to utilize a log-likelihood loss. In this instance, however, we have multiple classes and are operating in a continuous space. These are challenges that we should be aware of and whose results we will look at later.

For this example, we will be using the categorical cross-entropy loss function as well as another custom loss function. The former is native to Keras and is commonly used in classification schemes that include more than two classes.

When we run the preceding designed experiment, the results in this instance are uniformly quite bad. Across many different parameters and different styles, it is largely inadvisable to utilize policy gradients. With that in mind, let us try Deep Q Networks.

RL Approach 2: Deep Q Network

For this example, Q learning is definitely an excellent choice in terms of how we frame the problem, but Deep Q Learning ultimately should be the method that we choose. The reasoning behind this is the fact that the state space, particularly when considering the multitude of options, can be quite large. When we are running this part of the function, we should notice an output similar to Figure 4-6.

```
('Episode: 0', 'Total reward: -133.4', 'Loss: 0.00609607854858', 'Explore P: 0.9058')
('Episode: 1', 'Total reward: -115.6', 'Loss: 0.00257436116226', 'Explore P: 0.8205')
('Episode: 2', 'Total reward: -102.4', 'Loss: 0.000325706583681', 'Explore P: 0.7434')
('Episode: 3', 'Total reward: -98.0', 'Loss: 0.000310506671667', 'Explore P: 0.6736')
('Episode: 4', 'Total reward: 1383.0', 'Loss: 0.00124389817938', 'Explore P: 0.6105')
('Episode: 5', 'Total reward: -74.4', 'Loss: 0.000752292573452', 'Explore P: 0.5533')
('Episode: 6', 'Total reward: -63.4', 'Loss: 0.0001555577619', 'Explore P: 0.5016')
('Episode: 7', 'Total reward: -65.4', 'Loss: 0.000629861897323', 'Explore P: 0.4548')
('Episode: 8', 'Total reward: -58.4', 'Loss: 0.000218583256355', 'Explore P: 0.4125')
('Episode: 9', 'Total reward: -56.6', 'Loss: 0.000753238273319', 'Explore P: 0.3742')
('Episode: 10', 'Total reward: -46.2', 'Loss: 0.000115807146358', 'Explore P: 0.3395')
('Episode: 11', 'Total reward: -40.0', 'Loss: 0.000382943660952', 'Explore P: 0.3082')
('Episode: 12', 'Total reward: -35.0', 'Loss: 3.93268710468e-05', 'Explore P: 0.2798')
('Episode: 13', 'Total reward: -40.8', 'Loss: 0.000602947198786', 'Explore P: 0.2541')
('Episode: 14', 'Total reward: -31.0', 'Loss: 0.000622002757154', 'Explore P: 0.2309')
('Episode: 15', 'Total reward: -30.4', 'Loss: 4.48514838354e-05', 'Explore P: 0.2099')
('Episode: 16', 'Total reward: -24.8', 'Loss: 0.000435164460214', 'Explore P: 0.1909')
('Episode: 17', 'Total reward: -22.8', 'Loss: 0.000406970444601', 'Explore P: 0.1736')
('Episode: 18', 'Total reward: -24.6', 'Loss: 6.83790640323e-05', 'Explore P: 0.1581')
```

Figure 4-6. *Example Screenshot of Training DQL Model*

During training of several iterations, given the amount of data we have, I observed that training above one episode largely was inadvisable. With that being said, the results achieved at times were very inconsistent. On some iterations, I observed that the results were exceptionally good, some outcomes of the model would choose no actions at all, and some actions. On several occasions, I observed that the market making algorithm in this context did perform considerably well in training but those results were not stable nor consistent. Overwhelmingly, I noticed that my suggested model performed poorly more often than not and often got stuck making decisions that were undesirable. Moving forward however, let us look at the results when we repeat the out-of-sample experiment trials (Figure 4-7).

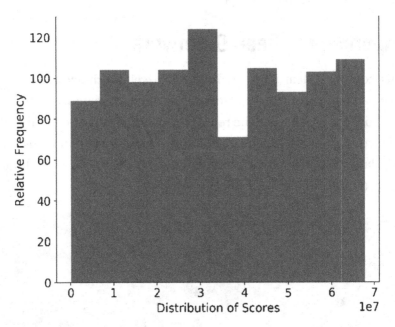

Figure 4-7. *Reward Score Distribution*

The preceding results are not only substantially better than the baseline but outstandingly outperform that of the policy gradient model, making this the obvious choice of selection. With an average reward of

34, 286, 348, this would absolutely be a feasible solution. As we can see in the plot in Figure 4-7, our scores are desirable and that we seem to have a bimodal distribution.

Results and Discussion

After reviewing all of the results, it is reasonable to state that readers should neither use the Deep Q Learning algorithm nor the policy gradients. In summary, these are the reasons we are suggesting this:

- **The baseline algorithm was exceeded** – In order to justify any experimental approach, we must exceed the baseline. It is worthwhile to inspect whether we are sampling the data appropriately, or if there is enough data for this particular.

- **Some algorithms lost money** – The most objective criticism of the first approach we have taken here is the fact that it did not achieve its business objectives, which was to produce a profitable strategy. Utilizing this algorithm in a business context would be inadvisable and ultimately beyond what theoretically works, we must choose what actually does.

Possible solutions moving forward are to read some of the existing literature that is in this space to try and remedy this. With that being said, many papers that are publicly available similarly ran into issues where algorithms either were momentarily profitable and ultimately not profitable. Readers should also feel free to try and apply ActorCritic methods in their own time moving forward, but should also be unafraid to also try other existing solutions and try different parameters, fee structures, and different constraints on the strategy that were not addressed here.

The difficulty of Reinforcement Learning research is that the reward function design is an abstract process, but with that being said a critical component to the design of good experiments.

Conclusion

With the following example complete, we now have reached the end of our first chapter in which we tackle reinforcement learning problems from scratch and try and improve upon existing methods. Some key takeaways from this chapter are the difficulties in trying to create a deployable solution, but proposing to the reader a framework and showing how we successively reached better results in sample each time suggested that we are getting closer to the answer. Prior to this point, many of the problems we have tackled have been relatively straightforward or classic examples whose value is being able to transparently show the power of the algorithm. Now we have finally gotten to the difficult part of the topic, which is learning to push the needle on various solutions. For those who are working directly in research or industry, this process should be familiar. If it is not, I highly suggest that you begin implementing this. With that being said, we will move on to the final chapter where we will repeat this process, but on a brand new environment, and we will walk the reader through how to create their own OpenAI gym environment from scratch so they can begin to do their own research on their own!

CHAPTER 5

Custom OpenAI Reinforcement Learning Environments

For our final chapter, we will be focusing on OpenAI's gym package, but more importantly trying to understand how we can create our own custom environments so we can tackle more than the typical use cases. Most of this chapter will focus around what I would suggest regarding programming practices for OpenAI as well as recommendations on how I would generally write most of this software. Finally, after we have completed creating an environment, we will move on to focusing on solving the problem. For this instance, we will focus on trying to create and solve a new video game.

Overview of Sonic the Hedgehog

For those who aren't familiar, *Sonic the Hedgehog* (Figure 5-1) is another classic game, often considered a rival to that of *Super Mario Bros*. The concept of the game is that you are playing a hedgehog that races from

© Taweh Beysolow II 2019
T. Beysolow II, *Applied Reinforcement Learning with Python*,
https://doi.org/10.1007/978-1-4842-5127-0_5

one side of the level to the other, with the objective of avoiding or killing enemies and collecting rings. If the player gets attacked, they lose all of their rings. If they get attacked with 0 rings, they lose a life. If they lose all of their lives, the game ends. We will not be focusing on any levels with boss battles for now and instead will focus on a simple introduction level (Level 1). As it relates to this task, our objective will to be to train the agent to successfully navigate the level without dying.

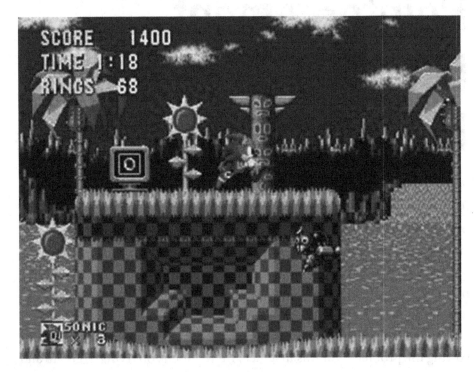

Figure 5-1. *Sonic the Hedgehog Screenshot*

Downloading the Game

Foremost, users will need to start by creating a Steam account and then downloading Steam to their local machine, if they have not done so already. For those not familiar, Steam is a game streaming service that allows players to buy and rent games without having to get a specific console. In this context, we will be buying *Sonic the Hedgehog* ($4.99). After the user has downloaded the game, they should see the following screen once they have logged into the Steam desktop client (Figure 5-2).

Figure 5-2. Steam Dashboard

After installing the game, readers should see the play button, indicating that the preliminary setup is done. However, there is some boiler plate which we need to do with the retro library that we will walk the reader through now. Retro is a library that specifically works with older video games and making them compatible with OpenAI. This will take care of a lot of the heavy lifting that we would otherwise encounter and make the process much more straightforward. Regardless, let us download the files we need accordingly. First, users should download and clone the repository at this URL: `https://github.com/openai/retro`.

After cloning this repository, we then need to create a virtual environment. For those that are not familiar, virtual environments are a way of created isolated instances of certain python installations and the relative dependencies associated with it. The benefit to this is that for isolated tasks, or projects, we can create python installations that have only the dependencies that they use. Once virtualenv is installed, we can instantiate it by entering the following commands into the bash terminal:

```
"sudo mkdir virtual_environments && cd virtual_environments"
"virtualenv [environment name]/python3 -m venv [environment name]"
```

These commands respectively create the virtual environment directory, cd into them, and then create the virtual environment. After this is completed, users should then cd into the directory where the locally cloned retro library sits. After that, they should type in the following command:

```
"python -m retro.import.sega_classics"
```

This command writes the respective ROMs for the games that fall underneath the sega_classics.py files to our local environment. ROM refers to read-only memory and usually in this context refers to the memory that stores video games that often was distributed via cartridges, the norm before the advent of discs and DVDs. Now that we have downloaded the game and its respective ROMs, let's move forward to how to work with retro and python to create a custom environment.

Writing the Code for the Environment

When looking back to the Super Mario Bros. and Doom examples, readers can reference the fact that we used a custom library that utilized some of the same techniques. Foremost let us analyze the functions in chapter5/create_environment.py and describe what each of these will be doing in detail. To begin, let us look at the body function as shown as follows:

```
def create_new_environment(environment_index, n_frames=4):
 (code redacted, please see github!)
    print(dictionary[environment_index]['game'])
```

```
print(dictionary[environment_index]['state'])

environment = make(game=dictionary[environment_index]['game'],

state=dictionary[environment_index]['state'],
bk2dir="./records")

environment = ActionsDiscretizer(environment)
environment = RewardScaler(environment)
environment = PreprocessFrame(environment)
environment = FrameStack(environment, n_frames)
environment = AllowBacktracking(environment)
return environment
```

The process of making an environment is fairly straightforward, in that we pass through parameters to the make() function from the "retro_contest" module. This creates an environment which we then add structure to from a variety of functions, until we eventually return back our customized and formatted environment. To begin, however, let us first talk about one of the most important aspects of our environment, which will be creating and defining the actions we can perform within them.

```
class PreprocessFrame(gym.ObservationWrapper):
def __init__(self, environment, width, height):
        gym.ObservationWrapper.__init__(self, environment)
        self.width = width
        self.height = height
        self.observation_space = gym.spaces.Box(low=0,
high=255,          •

shape=(self.height, self.width, 1),
dtype=np.uint8)

    def observation(self, image):
        image = cv2.cvtColor(image, cv2.COLOR_RGB2GRAY)
```

```
image = cv2.resize(image, (self.width, self.height),
interpolation=cv2.INTER_AREA)
image = image[:, :, None]
return image
```

Like most of the problems we have been dealing with when working
with 2D or 3D video games, we are essentially dealing with a permutation
of a computer vision problem. As such, we need to start by preprocessing
the image such that we reduce the input size or the neural network (or
other method) we will utilize, and then return a single one-dimensional
matrix of the grayscaled image. Most of this should be familiar to readers
from the prior chapters, but for posterity, we start by instantiating the
PreprocessFrame() class, which first accepts as its only argument the
ObservationWrapper. Readers have worked with this in every example
earlier, as evidenced from OpenAI Gym source code as follows:

```
class ObservationWrapper(Wrapper):
    def reset(self, **kwargs):
        observation = self.env.reset(**kwargs)
        return self.observation(observation)

    def step(self, action):
        observation, reward, done, info = self.env.step(action)
        return self.observation(observation), reward, done, info

    def observation(self, observation):
        raise NotImplementedError
```

This is the core of the library where we step, reset, and yield the current
state of the environment. Moving back to the PreprocessFrame() class,
we start by defining the environment, the width and the height of the
image we want to output. From these three arguments, we also define
observation space that we will have the ability to manipulate our agent
within. For this, we utilize the Box() class from gym. This is simply defined

as an element of Euclidean space in $\mathbb{R}^n$. In this instance, we would define the bounds of this box as 0 and 255, representing the degree of whiteness of a given pixel, where 0 is complete absence of whiteness (black) and 255 is the complete absence of darkness (white). The observation() function performs the actual grayscaling of an individual frame and outputting it so that we can analyze it. Moving forward, let us get into the meat and potatoes of creating an environment with the next class, the ActionsDiscretizer().

```
class ActionsDiscretizer(gym.ActionWrapper):
def __init__(self, env):
        super(ActionsDiscretizer, self).__init__(env)
        buttons = ["B", "A", "MODE", "START", "UP", "DOWN",
        "LEFT", "RIGHT", "C", "Y", "X", "Z"]
        actions = [['LEFT'], ['RIGHT'], ['LEFT', 'DOWN'],
        ['RIGHT', 'DOWN'], ['DOWN'],
                    ['DOWN', 'B'], ['B']]
        self._actions = []
```

Starting with the instantiation of the class, readers should direct themselves to the buttons and actions array. Depending on whether you are designing an environment for a keyboard or for a specific game console, the buttons will differ. These buttons correspond to all of the possible buttons on a Sega Genesis controller.

With that being said, not every possible action will map to every button, particularly in the case of this version of *Sonic the Hedgehog*. Although certain advanced capabilities were added with newer iterations of the game, the original game is pretty standard in that Sonic can walk/run left or right and can jump using the "B" button. Moving forward, let us look at how we create a specific action space.

```
for action in actions:
        _actions = np.array([False] * len(buttons))
        for button in action:
            _actions[buttons.index(button)] = True
        self._actions.append(_actions)
    self.action_space = gym.spaces.Discrete(len(self._actions))
```

For the array of actions, we then iterate through each of the actions in the "actions" array and then create a new array entitled "_actions." This should be an array with dimensions 1 x N where N is the number of buttons on the controller and every index is false. Now, for each of the buttons in the actions, we want to map that to an array where some entries will be False and others True. Finally, this is assigned to "action_space" as an attribute of the "self" variable. We have already discussed scaling rewards other times, so there is no need to review that function. However, we should discuss an important function, particularly in games/environments similar to this one.

```
class AllowBacktracking(gym.Wrapper):
def __init__(self, environment):
        super(AllowBacktracking, self).__init__(environment)
        self.curent_reward = 0
        self.max_reward = 0

    def reset(self, **kwargs):
        self.current_reward = 0
        self.max_reward = 0
        return self.env.reset(**kwargs)
```

The AllowBacktracting() class is fairly simple in that for 2D environments, we must reach the end of the level by going backward eventually. With that being stated, however, sometimes, it is possible that there is a better path to be taken if we occasionally (however minor) backtrack our steps and then chose and alternative set of actions. We don't want to encourage the reward structure to do this too much, however, so we assign the following step function to the environment:

```
def step(self, action):
    observation, reward, done, info = self.environment.
    step(action)
    self.current_reward += reward
    reward = max(0, self.current_reward - self.max_reward)
    self.max_reward = max(self.max_reward, self.current_
    reward)
    return observation, reward, done, info
```

The important part for the reader to take away from this function is the fact that we are assigning the reward value to be 0 or above 0. In that case, we are not going to go backward if it results in a poor reward. With all of the boilerplate done, let us move onward to discussing what model we will be using specifically and why.

A3C Actor-Critic

Readers will recall that we utilized this model when trying to train our agent to play *Super Mario Bros.*; we utilized the Advantage Actor-Critic model which was abbreviated as A2C. In Figure 5-3, we can see a visualization of an A3C Network.

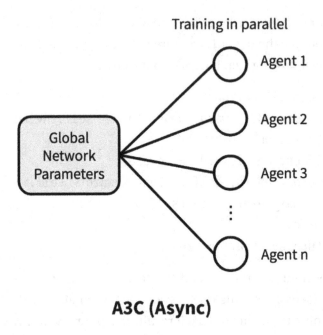

Figure 5-3. *A3C Diagram*

As stated earlier, Actor-Critic networks are effective in the sense that we are able to use the value function to update the policy function. Rather than waiting for an episode to finish and taking all of the actions, regardless of which individual ones were good vs. bad, we can incrementally evaluate each action and then change our policy accordingly to receive a much more optimized result and quicker than using vanilla policy gradients. With respect to A3C vs. A2C, A3C tends to be less optimal because we are training multiple agents parallel to one another all based off of some set of initial global parameters. Each agent, as it explores the environment, will update the parameters accordingly, from which other agents will update. However, not all agents will update at the same time, hence the "asynchronous" nature of this problem. Moving forward, however, let us discuss our implementation as it is contained in the A3CModel() class.

```
class A3CNetwork():

    def __init__(self, s_size, a_size, scope, trainer):
        (code redacted)
layer3 = tf.layers.flatten(inputs=layer3)

            output_layer = fully_connected_layer(inputs=layer3,
            units=512,
activation='softmax')

            outputs, cell_state, hidden_state = lstm_
layer(input=hidden,
size=s_size,
actions=a_size,
apply_softmax=False)
```

Similar to the A2C solution we deployed earlier, we start by passing through a preprocessed image through convolutional layers. This helps us to reduce dimensionality and also remove noise from the data as stated earlier. However a new step we will feature here that wasn't in the prior example will be to pass the data through an LSTM layer. LSTMs were models devised in the 1990s by Sepp Hochreiter and Jürgen Schmidhuber, the long short-term memory unit, or LSTM. Let us start by visualizing what this model looks like as it is detailed in the image shown in Figure 5-4.

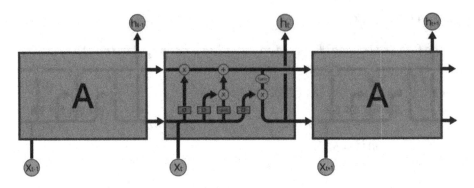

Figure 5-4. *LSTM Model*

LSTMs are distinguished structurally by the fact that we observe them as blocks, or units, rather than the traditional structure we often see a neural network appearing as. With that being said, the same principles are generally applied here. However, we have an improvement over the hidden state from the vanilla RNN that we discussed earlier that we will begin walking through the formulae associated with the LSTM:

$$i_t = \sigma\left(W_{xi}x_t + W_{hi}h_{t-1} + W_{hc}c_{t-1} + b_i\right) \tag{2.12}$$

$$f_t = \sigma\left(W_{xf}x_t + W_{hf}h_{t-1} + W_{hf}c_{t-1} + b_f\right) \tag{2.13}$$

$$c_t = f_t \circ c_{t-1} + i_t \circ \tanh\left(W_{xc}x_t + W_{hc}h_{t-1} + b_c\right) \tag{2.14}$$

$$o_t = \sigma\left(W_{xo}x_t + W_{ho}h_{t-1} + W_{co}c_t + b_o\right) \tag{2.15}$$

$$h_t = o_t \circ \tanh\left(c_t\right) \tag{2.16}$$

where i_t is the input gate, f_t is the forget gate, c_t is the cell state, o_t is the output gate, h_t is the output vector, σ is the sigmoid activation function, and tanh is the tanh activation function.

Initially, let us draw our attention to the diagram of the model, specifically the LSTM unit in the center, and understand the directional flow as they relate to the formulae. Preliminarily, let us discuss the notation. Each block, denoted by rectangles [   ], represents a neural network layer, through which we pass through values. The horizontal lines with arrows represent the vectors and direction in which the data moves. The data, after it moves through a neural network layer, often is passed to a pointwise operation object, represented by circles ◯. Both the hidden and cell states are initialized at 0 upon initialization of the algorithm. Programmatically, most of the computation associated with the LSTM layer happens underneath the hood of the "dynamic_rnn()" function that is supplied by Tensorflow; however, we create a body function around this function where the preceding cells, states, and associated variables are defined as follows:

```
def lstm_layer(input, size, actions, apply_softmax=False):
    input = tf.expand_dims(input, [0])
    lstm = tf.contrib.rnn.BasicLSTMCell(size, state_is_
    tuple=True)
    state_size = lstm.state_size
    step_size = tf.shape(input)[:1]
    cell_init = np.zeros((1, state_size.c), np.float32)
    hidden_init = np.zeros((1, state_size.h), np.float32)
    initial_state = [cell_init, hidden_init]
    cell_state = tf.placeholder(tf.float32, [1, state_size.c])
    hidden_state = tf.placeholder(tf.float32, [1, state_size.h])
    input_state = tf.contrib.rnn.LSTMStateTuple(cell_state,
    hidden_state)
    (code redacted, please see github!)
```

Specifically as to where and when an LSTM model is utilized, it is most common for them to be applied to sequence-based tasks where a given output depends on more than one input. Examples of this might be tasks such as spell check, translating languages, and predicting time series. As it relates to this specific task, we are preprocessing the data such that we stack frames four at a time. This is typically done to try and simulate some form of motion where we determine the best possible action to take based on several prior observations. In this instance, the reasoning behind why an RNN would be applied is straightforward. While an LSTM is not necessary, we thought it useful to show the reader how we can combine additional and differing types of machine learning models to this problem. Moving forward, let us direct our attention back to the A3C network itself and move toward the latter part of the function.

```
self.policy = slim.fully_connected(output_layer,
a_size,
    activation_fn=tf.nn.softmax,
    weights_initializer=normalized_columns_
    initializer(0.01),
    biases_initializer=None)

self.value = slim.fully_connected(rnn_out, 1,
    activation_fn=None,
    weights_initializer=normalized_columns_
    initializer(1.0),
    biases_initializer=None)
```

With the output from the LSTM yielded, we pass this through a fully connected layer such that we now have defined our policy and value functions, which we will utilize moving forward to produce an output matrix. Separately, readers should observe the calculation of the gradient and update to the parameters to individually be similar. However, what precisely makes this model different is the asynchronous nature of the works. Now, we will walk through the final portion of code, which will be what we can refer to as the main/master function.

```
def play_sonic()
(code redacted, please see github!)
wiith tf.device("/cpu:0"):
```

```
master_network = AC_Network(s_size,a_size,'global',None)
num_workers = multiprocessing.cpu_count()
workers = []

for i in range(num_workers):

    workers.append(Worker(environment=environment,
                          name=i,
                          s_size=s_size,
                          a_sizse=a_size,
                          trainer=trainer,
                          saver=saver,
                          model_path=model_path))
```

In the following code, we start by creating the master network, which contains the global parameters and creating a number of workers based on the available CPUs. The previously shown method will ensure that we do not utilize more memory than we should and crash the program. Then for each of the workers we intend to create, we append them to an array after we instantiate them. Moving forward, however, is where the important part of the computation happens.

```
coord = tf.train.Coordinator()
sess.run(tf.global_variables_initializer())
worker_threads = []

    for worker in workers:

        worker_work = lambda: worker.work(max_episode_
        length=max_episode_length,
        gamma=gamma,
        master_network=master_network,
        sess=sess,
        coord=coord)
```

```
            _thread = threading.Thread(target=(worker_work))
            _thread.start()
            worker_threads.append(_thread)
        coord.join(worker_threads)
```

Readers should first take note of the tf.train.Coordinator() function that we will be using as well as the threading library. For the implementation of A3C, it is important to understand what we are doing on the backend to clear any potential confusion up. For those that are unaware, a thread is an individual flow of execution such that multithreading would allow you to run processes on different processors. We create a thread with the "_thread" variable by passing it a function, in this case, the "worker_work" variable. This is created by the worker.work() function, which we define as the following body of code:

```
    def work(self,max_episode_length,gamma,sess,coord,saver):
        (code redacted, please see github!)
while self.env.is_episode_finished() == False:
action_dist, value_function ,rnn_state = sess.run([self.local_
AC.policy,
            self.local_AC.value,
self.local_AC.state_out]...)}

                action = np.random.choice(action_dist[0],
                p=action_dist[0])
                action = np.argmax(action_dist == action)

                reward = self.env.make_action(self.
                actions[action]) / 100.0
                done = self.env.is_episode_finished()
episode_buffer.append([prior_state, action, reward, current_
state, done, value[0,0]])
                episode_values.append(value[0,0])
```

We start by first instantiating a couple of variables by executing the computational graph/A3C model. Specifically, in the preceding section of code we want to randomly choose actions from the distribution that is yielded. From this point, everything else should seem relatively familiar from prior examples. We perform an action in the environment, which should yield some reward and also a value function. What is new to the reader, however, is how we would update the master parameters for the workers. This itself ties back into the multithreading example, specifically with the coord.join() function. With an understanding of threading and where this ties into the implementation of A3C as we have written it, we can finally discuss the tf.train.Coodinator() function we briefly brought up earlier. This function is utilized to coordinate the termination of multiple threads once they have all terminated. This is specifically done with the join() function, which we use when we want one thread to wait for another to finish. This will cause the main thread to pause and wait for another thread to complete. **This** is precisely where the asynchronous nature of A3C comes to life in this problem!

Conclusion

When training the model for 10 hours, we observed reasonable performance; however, something that tends to continuously be a problem is the parts of the level where Sonic needs to oftentimes run around the circular paths. Because of this, more training is likely recommended. With that being said, initially we have noticed the ability of the agent to defeat or avoid enemies as well as the ability to move through the level while collecting some coins. With this being stated though, this sheds light on the difficulty of this problem.

Readers must be aware of the difficulty of reinforcement learning. While RL is still a heavily researched field, for those that want to deploy these for solutions should be aware that Actor-Critic models in particular can be very difficult to write from scratch. Not even addressing the models themselves, we spent a significant bit of time building the boilerplate to even handle the environment. While this was a simple 2D game, there are fairly complex environments that would merit working alongside and engineer who focused entirely on building the tools to render and wrap the environment.

With respect to solving the problem itself, the amount of time taken to train without an indication of precisely how the problem should be tackled can result in a large amount of wasted time. Frame your problems appropriately and be prepared to try many different methods, but spend far more time in the instance of reinforcement learning framing the problem than you would try different approaches. Moreover, when you're designing your environments, consider what the different reward structures you could utilize. For example, in the instance of Sonic, do you want to preference picking up more rings than less, or is it better to preference gaining points from destroying enemies? Obviously, in the instance of dying, that should be what yields the largest negative reward, but is it worst to die in your eyes from Sonic falling off the map or worse to die from getting killed by a random enemy? All of these considerations will affect training but should be high-level concerns that should be addressed at the beginning of the problem.

Readers are encouraged to utilize the code provided in these examples and improve on them where they see fit, perhaps by making certain implementations more computationally efficient and also where it is appropriate to improve upon the solutions as they were presented. With collaboration, we can solve problems of incredible difficulty and drive this field forward together.

APPENDIX A

Source Code

This appendix references the initial release source code for this book. For updates that will happen occasionally to the code base as necessary, please check the Github by going to www.apress.com/9781484251263.

Market Making Model Utilities

```python
from collections import deque

class Memory():

    def __init__(self, max_size):
        self.buffer = deque(maxlen = max_size)

    def add(self, experience):
        self.buffer.append(experience)

    def sample(self, batch_size):
        buffer_size = len(self.buffer)
        index = np.random.choice(np.arange(buffer_size),
                                  size=batch_size,
                                  replace=True)

        return [self.buffer[i] for i in index]

class DeepQNetworkMM():
```

© Taweh Beysolow II 2019
T. Beysolow II, *Applied Reinforcement Learning with Python*,
https://doi.org/10.1007/978-1-4842-5127-0

```python
def __init__(self, n_units, n_classes, state_size, action_
size, learning_rate):
    self.state_size = state_size
    self.action_size = action_size
    self.learning_rate = learning_rate
    self.n_units = n_units
    self.n_classes = n_classes

    self.input_matrix = tf.placeholder(tf.float32,
    [None, state_size])
    self.actions = tf.placeholder(tf.float32,
    [None, n_classes])
    self.target_Q = tf.placeholder(tf.float32, [None])

    self.layer1 = fully_connected_layer(inputs=self.input_
    matrix, units=self.n_units, activation='selu')

    self.hidden_layer = fully_connected_layer(inputs=self.
    layer1, units=self.n_units, activation='selu')

    self.output_layer = fully_connected_layer(inputs=self.
    hidden_layer, units=n_classes, activation=None)

    self.predicted_Q = tf.reduce_sum(tf.multiply(self.
    output_layer, self.actions), axis=1)

    self.error_rate = tf.reduce_mean(tf.square(self.
    target_Q - self.predicted_Q))

    self.optimizer = tf.train.RMSPropOptimizer(self.
    learning_rate).minimize(self.error_rate)
```

Policy Gradient Utilities

```python
import keras.layers as layers
from keras import backend
from keras.models import Model
from keras.optimizers import Adam
from keras.initializers import glorot_uniform
class PolicyGradient():

    def __init__(self, n_units, n_layers, n_columns, n_outputs,
    learning_rate, hidden_activation, output_activation, loss_
    function):
        self.n_units = n_units
        self.n_layers = n_layers
        self.n_columns = n_columns
        self.n_outputs = n_outputs
        self.hidden_activation = hidden_activation
        self.output_activation = output_activation
        self.learning_rate = learning_rate
        self.loss_function = loss_function

    def create_policy_model(self, input_shape):
        input_layer = layers.Input(shape=input_shape)
        advantages = layers.Input(shape=[1])

        hidden_layer = layers.Dense(units=self.n_units,
        activation=self.hidden_activation, use_bias=False,
        kernel_initializer=glorot_uniform(seed=42))(input_
        layer)

        output_layer = layers.Dense(units=self.n_outputs,
        activation=self.output_activation,  use_bias=False,
        kernel_initializer=glorot_uniform(seed=42))(hidden_
        layer)
```

```
def log_likelihood_loss(actual_labels, predicted_labels):
    log_likelihood = backend.log(actual_labels *
    (actual_labels - predicted_labels) + (1 - actual_
    labels) * (actual_labels + predicted_labels))
    return backend.mean(log_likelihood * advantages,
    keepdims=True)

if self.loss_function == 'log_likelihood':
    self.loss_function = log_likelihood_loss
else:
    self.loss_function = 'categorical_crossentropy'

policy_model = Model(inputs=[input_layer, advantages],
outputs=output_layer)
policy_model.compile(loss=self.loss_function,
optimizer=Adam(self.learning_rate))
model_prediction = Model(input=[input_layer],
outputs=output_layer)
return policy_model, model_prediction
```

Models

```
import tensorflow as tf, numpy as np
from baselines.common.distributions import make_pdtype

activation_dictionary = {'elu': tf.nn.elu,
                         'relu': tf.nn.relu,
                         'selu': tf.nn.selu,
                         'sigmoid': tf.nn.sigmoid,
                         'softmax': tf.nn.softmax,
                         None: None}
```

```
def normalized_columns_initializer(standard_deviation=1.0):
  def initializer(shape, dtype=None, partition_info=None):
    output = np.random.randn(*shape).astype(np.float32)
    output *= standard_deviation/float(np.sqrt(np.
    square(output).sum(axis=0, keepdims=True)))
    return tf.constant(output)
  return initializer

def linear_operation(x, size, name, initializer=None, bias_
init=0):
  with tf.variable_scope(name):
    weights = tf.get_variable("w", [x.get_shape()[1], size],
    initializer=initializer)
    biases = tf.get_variable("b", [size], initializer=tf.
    constant_initializer(bias_init))
    return tf.matmul(x, weights) + biases
def convolution_layer(inputs, dimensions, filters, kernel_size,
strides, gain=np.sqrt(2), activation='relu'):

    if dimensions == 3:

        return tf.layers.conv1d(inputs=inputs,
                                filters=filters,
                                kernel_size=kernel_size,
                                kernel_initializer=tf.
                                orthogonal_initializer(gain),
                                strides=(strides),
                                activation=activation_
                                dictionary[activation])
```

```
    elif dimensions == 4:

        return tf.layers.conv2d(inputs=inputs,
                                filters=filters,
                                kernel_size=kernel_size,
                                kernel_initializer=tf.
                                orthogonal_initializer(gain),
                                strides=(strides),
                                activation=activation_
                                dictionary[activation])

def fully_connected_layer(inputs, units, activation, gain=np.
sqrt(2)):
    return tf.layers.dense(inputs=inputs,
                           units=units,
                           activation=activation_
                           dictionary[activation],
                           kernel_initializer=tf.orthogonal_
                           initializer(gain))

def lstm_layer(input, size, actions, apply_softmax=False):
    input = tf.expand_dims(input, [0])
    lstm = tf.contrib.rnn.BasicLSTMCell(size, state_is_
    tuple=True)
    state_size = lstm.state_size
    step_size = tf.shape(input)[:1]
    cell_init = np.zeros((1, state_size.c), np.float32)
    hidden_init = np.zeros((1, state_size.h), np.float32)
    initial_state = [cell_init, hidden_init]
    cell_state = tf.placeholder(tf.float32, [1, state_size.c])
    hidden_state = tf.placeholder(tf.float32, [1, state_size.h])
    input_state = tf.contrib.rnn.LSTMStateTuple(cell_state,
    hidden_state)
```

```python
    _outputs, states = tf.nn.dynamic_rnn(cell=lstm,
                                inupts=input,
                                initial_state=input_
                                state,
                                sequence_length=step_size,
                                time_major=False)
    _cell_state, _hidden_state = states
    output = tf.reshape(_outputs, [-1, size])
    output_state = [_cell_state[:1, :], _hidden_state[:1, :]]
    output = linear_operation(output, actions, "logits",
    normalized_columns_initializer(0.01))
    output = tf.nn.softmax(output, dim=-1)
    return output, _cell_state, _hidden_state
def create_weights_biases(n_layers, n_units, n_columns, n_outputs):
    '''

    Creates dictionaries of variable length for differing
    neural network models

    Arguments

    n_layers - int - number of layers
    n_units - int - number of neurons within each individual
    layer
    n_columns - int - number of columns within dataset

    :return: dict (int), dict (int)
    '''

    weights, biases = {}, {}
    for i in range(n_layers):
        if i == 0:
            weights['layer'+str(i)] = tf.Variable(tf.random_
            normal([n_columns, n_units]))
```

```
            biases['layer'+str(i)] = tf.Variable(tf.random_
            normal([n_columns]))
        elif i != 0 and i != n_layers-1:
            weights['layer'+str(i)] = tf.Variable(tf.random_
            normal([n_units, n_units]))
            biases['layer'+str(i)] = tf.Variable(tf.random_
            normal([n_units]))
        elif i != 0 and i == n_layers-1:
            weights['output_layer'] = tf.Variable(tf.random_
            normal([n_units, n_outputs]))
            biases['output_layer'] = tf.Variable(tf.random_
            normal([n_outputs]))

    return weights, biases
def create_input_output(input_dtype, output_dtype, n_columns,
n_outputs):
    '''

    Create placeholder variables for tensorflow graph

    '''

    X = tf.placeholder(shape=(None, n_columns), dtype=input_dtype)
    Y = tf.placeholder(shape=(None, n_outputs), dtype=output_dtype)
    return X, Y

class DeepQNetwork():

    def __init__(self, n_units, n_classes, n_filters, stride,
    kernel, state_size, action_size, learning_rate):
        self.state_size = state_size
        self.action_size = action_size
        self.learning_rate = learning_rate
        self.n_units = n_units
```

```
self.n_classes = n_classes
self.n_filters = n_filters
self.stride = stride
self.kernel = kernel

self.input_matrix = tf.placeholder(tf.float32,
[None, state_size])
self.actions = tf.placeholder(tf.float32,
[None, n_classes])
self.target_Q = tf.placeholder(tf.float32, [None])

self.network1 = convolution_layer(inputs=self.input_
matrix,
                                  filters=self.n_filters,
                                  kernel_size=self.kernel,
                                  strides=self.stride,
                                  dimensions=4,
                                  activation='elu')

self.network1 = tf.layers.batch_normalization(self.
network1, training=True, epsilon=1e-5)
self.network2 = convolution_layer(inputs=self.network1,
                                  filters=self.n_filters*2,
                                  kernel_size=int(self.
                                  kernel/2),
                                  strides=int(self.stride/2),
                                  dimensions=4,
                                  activation='elu')

self.network2 = tf.layers.batch_
normalization(inputs=self.network2, training=True,
epsilon=1e-5)
```

```
        self.network3 = convolution_layer(inputs=self.network2,
                                  filters=self.n_filters*4,
                                  kernel_size=int(self.
                                  kernel/2),
                                  strides=int(self.
                                  stride/2), dimensions=4,
                                  activation='elu')

    self.network3 = tf.layers.batch_
    normalization(inputs=self.network3, training=True,
    epsilon=1e-5)

    self.network3 = tf.layers.flatten(inputs=self.network3)

    self.output = fully_connected_layer(inputs=self.network3,
                                    units=self.n_units,
                                     activation='elu')

    self.output = fully_connected_layer(inputs=self.output,
                          units=n_classes, activation=None)

    self.predicted_Q = tf.reduce_sum(tf.multiply(self.
    output, self.actions), axis=1)

    self.error_rate = tf.reduce_mean(tf.square(self.
    target_Q - self.predicted_Q))

    self.optimizer = tf.train.RMSPropOptimizer(self.
    learning_rate).minimize(self.error_rate)

class ActorCriticModel():

    def __init__(self, session, environment, action_space,
    n_batches, n_steps, reuse=False):
```

```
session.run(tf.global_variables_initializer())
self.distribution_type = make_pdtype(action_space)
height, weight, channel = environment.shape
inputs_ = tf.placeholder(tf.float32, [height, weight,
channel], name='inputs')
scaled_images = tf.cast(inputs_, tf.float32)/float(255)

with tf.variable_scope('model', reuse=reuse):
    layer1 = tf.layers.batch_normalization(convolution_
    layer(inputs=scaled_images,
  filters=32,
  kernel_size=8,
  strides=4,
  dimensions=3))

    layer2 = tf.layers.batch_normalization(convolution_
    layer(inputs=tf.nn.relu(layer1),
  filters=64,
  kernel_size=4,
  strides=2,
  dimensions=3))

    layer3 = tf.layers.batch_normalization(convolution_
    layer(inputs=tf.nn.relu(layer2),
  filters=64,
  kernel_size=3,
  strides=1,
  dimensions=3))

    layer3 = tf.layers.flatten(inputs=layer3)
    output_layer = fully_connected_layer(inputs=layer3,
    units=512, activation='softmax')
```

```
        self.distribution, self.logits = self.distribution_
        type.pdfromlatent(output_layer, init_scale=0.01)
        value_function = fully_connected_layer(output_
        layer, units=1, activation=None)[:, 0]

    self.initial_state = None
    sampled_action = self.distribution.sample()

    def step(current_state, *_args, **_kwargs):
        action, value = session.run([sampled_action, value_
        function], {inputs_: current_state})
        return action, value

    def value(current_state, *_args, **_kwargs):
        return session.run(value_function, {inputs_:
        current_state})

    def select_action(current_state, *_args, **_kwargs):
        return session.run(sampled_action, {inputs_:
        current_state})
    self.inputs_ = inputs_
    self.value_function = value_function
    self.step = step
    self.value = value
    self.select_action = select_action
```

Chapter 1
OpenAI Example

```python
import gym

def cartpole():
    environment = gym.make('CartPole-v1')
    environment.reset()
    for _ in range(1000):
        environment.render()
        action = environment.action_space.sample()
        observation, reward, done, info = environment.
        step(action)
        print("Step {}:".format(_))
        print("action: {}".format(action))
        print("observation: {}".format(observation))
        print("reward: {}".format(reward))
        print("done: {}".format(done))
        print("info: {}".format(info))

if __name__ == '__main__':

    cartpole()
```

Chapter 2
Cart Pole Example

```python
import gym, numpy as np, matplotlib.pyplot as plt
from neural_networks.policy_gradient_utilities import
PolicyGradient

#Parameters
```

```python
n_units = 5
gamma = .99
batch_size = 50
learning_rate = 1e-3
n_episodes = 10000
render = False
goal = 190
n_layers = 2
n_classes = 2
environment = gym.make('CartPole-v1')
environment_dimension = len(environment.reset())

def calculate_discounted_reward(reward, gamma=gamma):
    output = [reward[i] * gamma**i for i in range(0,
len(reward))]
    return output[::-1]

def score_model(model, n_tests, render=render):
    scores = []
    for _ in range(n_tests):
        environment.reset()
        observation = environment.reset()
        reward_sum = 0
        while True:
            if render:
                environment.render()

            state = np.reshape(observation, [1, environment_
            dimension])
            predict = model.predict([state])[0]
            action = np.argmax(predict)
            observation, reward, done, _ = environment.
            step(action)
```

```
            reward_sum += reward
            if done:
                break
        scores.append(reward_sum)

    environment.close()
    return np.mean(scores)
def cart_pole_game(environment, policy_model, model_
predictions):
    loss = []
    n_episode, reward_sum, score, episode_done = 0, 0, 0, False
    n_actions = environment.action_space.n
    observation = environment.reset()

    states = np.empty(0).reshape(0, environment_dimension)
    actions = np.empty(0).reshape(0, 1)
    rewards = np.empty(0).reshape(0, 1)
    discounted_rewards = np.empty(0).reshape(0, 1)

    while n_episode < n_episodes:

        state = np.reshape(observation, [1, environment_
        dimension])
        prediction = model_predictions.predict([state])[0]
        action = np.random.choice(range(environment.action_
        space.n), p=prediction)
        states = np.vstack([states, state])
        actions = np.vstack([actions, action])

        observation, reward, episode_done, info = environment.
        step(action)
        reward_sum += reward
        rewards = np.vstack([rewards, reward])
```

```
if episode_done == True:

    discounted_reward = calculate_discounted_
    reward(rewards)
    discounted_rewards = np.vstack([discounted_rewards,
    discounted_reward])
    rewards = np.empty(0).reshape(0, 1)

    if (n_episode + 1) % batch_size == 0:

        discounted_rewards -= discounted_rewards.mean()
        discounted_rewards /= discounted_rewards.std()
        discounted_rewards = discounted_rewards.squeeze()
        actions = actions.squeeze().astype(int)

        train_actions = np.zeros([len(actions), n_actions])
        train_actions[np.arange(len(actions)), actions] = 1

        error = policy_model.train_on_batch([states,
        discounted_rewards], train_actions)
        loss.append(error)

        states = np.empty(0).reshape(0, environment_
        dimension)
        actions = np.empty(0).reshape(0, 1)
        discounted_rewards = np.empty(0).reshape(0, 1)

        score = score_model(model=model_predictions,
        n_tests=10)

        print('''\nEpisode: %s \nAverage Reward: %s  \
        nScore: %s \nError: %s'''
                )%(n_episode+1, reward_sum/float(batch_
                size), score, np.mean(loss[-batch_
                size:]))
```

```python
            if score >= goal:
                break

            reward_sum = 0

        n_episode += 1
        observation = environment.reset()

    plt.title('Policy Gradient Error plot over %s Episodes'%(n_
    episode+1))
    plt.xlabel('N batches')
    plt.ylabel('Error Rate')
    plt.plot(loss)
    plt.show()

if __name__ == '__main__':

    mlp_model = PolicyGradient(n_units=n_units,
                               n_layers=n_layers,
                               n_columns=environment_dimension,
                               n_outputs=n_classes,
                               learning_rate=learning_rate,
                               hidden_activation='selu',
                               output_activation='softmax',
                               loss_function='log_likelihood')

    policy_model, model_predictions = mlp_model.create_policy_
    model(input_shape=(environment_dimension, ))

    policy_model.summary()

    cart_pole_game(environment=environment,
                   policy_model=policy_model,
                   model_predictions=model_predictions)
```

Super Mario Example

```
import gym, numpy as np, matplotlib.pyplot as plt
from neural_networks.policy_gradient_utilities import
PolicyGradient

#Parameters
n_units = 5
gamma = .99
batch_size = 50
learning_rate = 1e-3
n_episodes = 10000
render = False
goal = 190
n_layers = 2
n_classes = 2
environment = gym.make('CartPole-v1')
environment_dimension = len(environment.reset())

def calculate_discounted_reward(reward, gamma=gamma):
    output = [reward[i] * gamma**i for i in range(0,
    len(reward))]
    return output[::-1]

def score_model(model, n_tests, render=render):
    scores = []
    for _ in range(n_tests):
        environment.reset()
        observation = environment.reset()
        reward_sum = 0
        while True:
            if render:
                environment.render()
```

```
        state = np.reshape(observation, [1, environment_
        dimension])
        predict = model.predict([state])[0]
        action = np.argmax(predict)
        observation, reward, done, _ = environment.step(action)
        reward_sum += reward
        if done:
            break
    scores.append(reward_sum)

environment.close()
return np.mean(scores)

def cart_pole_game(environment, policy_model, model_
predictions):
    loss = []
    n_episode, reward_sum, score, episode_done = 0, 0, 0, False
    n_actions = environment.action_space.n
    observation = environment.reset()

    states = np.empty(0).reshape(0, environment_dimension)
    actions = np.empty(0).reshape(0, 1)
    rewards = np.empty(0).reshape(0, 1)
    discounted_rewards = np.empty(0).reshape(0, 1)

    while n_episode < n_episodes:

        state = np.reshape(observation, [1, environment_
        dimension])
        prediction = model_predictions.predict([state])[0]
        action = np.random.choice(range(environment.action_
        space.n), p=prediction)
        states = np.vstack([states, state])
        actions = np.vstack([actions, action])
```

```
observation, reward, episode_done, info = environment.
step(action)
reward_sum += reward
rewards = np.vstack([rewards, reward])

if episode_done == True:

    discounted_reward = calculate_discounted_
    reward(rewards)
    discounted_rewards = np.vstack([discounted_rewards,
    discounted_reward])
    rewards = np.empty(0).reshape(0, 1)

    if (n_episode + 1) % batch_size == 0:

        discounted_rewards -= discounted_rewards.mean()
        discounted_rewards /= discounted_rewards.std()
        discounted_rewards = discounted_rewards.squeeze()
        actions = actions.squeeze().astype(int)

        train_actions = np.zeros([len(actions), n_actions])
        train_actions[np.arange(len(actions)), actions] = 1

        error = policy_model.train_on_batch([states,
        discounted_rewards], train_actions)
        loss.append(error)

        states = np.empty(0).reshape(0, environment_
        dimension)
        actions = np.empty(0).reshape(0, 1)
        discounted_rewards = np.empty(0).reshape(0, 1)

        score = score_model(model=model_predictions,
        n_tests=10)
```

```python
        print('''\nEpisode: %s \nAverage Reward: %s  \
        nScore: %s \nError: %s'''
              )%(n_episode+1, reward_sum/float(batch_
              size), score, np.mean(loss[-batch_size:]))

        if score >= goal:
            break

        reward_sum = 0

    n_episode += 1
    observation = environment.reset()

plt.title('Policy Gradient Error plot over %s Episodes'%(n_
episode+1))
plt.xlabel('N batches')
plt.ylabel('Error Rate')
plt.plot(loss)
plt.show()

if __name__ == '__main__':

    mlp_model = PolicyGradient(n_units=n_units,
                               n_layers=n_layers,
                               n_columns=environment_dimension,
                               n_outputs=n_classes,
                               learning_rate=learning_rate,
                               hidden_activation='selu',
                               output_activation='softmax',
                               loss_function='log_likelihood')

    policy_model, model_predictions = mlp_model.create_policy_
    model(input_shape=(environment_dimension, ))

    policy_model.summary()
```

```
cart_pole_game(environment=environment,
              policy_model=policy_model,
              model_predictions=model_predictions)
```

Chapter 3

Frozen Lake Example

```
import os, time, gym, numpy as np

#Parameters
learning_rate = 1e-2
gamma = 0.96
epsilon = 0.9
n_episodes = 10000
max_steps = 100
environment = gym.make('FrozenLake-v0')
Q_matrix = np.zeros((environment.observation_space.n,
environment.action_space.n))

def choose_action(state):
    '''

    To be used after Q table has been updated, returns an action

    Parameters:

        state - int - the current state of the agent

    :return: int
    '''

    return np.argmax(Q_matrix[state, :])
def exploit_explore(prior_state, epsilon=epsilon, Q_matrix=Q_
matrix):
    '''
```

One half of the exploit-explore paradigm that we will
utilize

Parameters

  prior_state - int - the prior state of the environment
  at a given iteration
  epsilon - float - parameter that we use to determine
  whether we will try a new or current best action

:return: int
'''

```
if np.random.uniform(0, 1) < epsilon:
    return environment.action_space.sample()
else:
    return np.argmax(Q_matrix[prior_state, :])
def update_q_matrix(prior_state, observation , reward, action):
    '''
```

Algorithm that updates the values in the Q table to reflect
knowledge acquired by the agent

Parameters

  prior_state - int - the prior state of the environment
  before the current timestemp
  observation - int - the current state of the
  environment
  reward - int - the reward yielded from the environment
  after an action
  action - int - the action suggested by the epsilon
  greedy algorithm

:return: None
'''

```python
    prediction = Q_matrix[prior_state, action]
    actual_label = reward + gamma * np.max(Q_
    matrix[observation, :])
    Q_matrix[prior_state, action] = Q_matrix[prior_state,
    action] + learning_rate*(actual_label - prediction)

def populate_q_matrix(render=False, n_episodes=n_episodes):
    '''
    Directly implementing Q Learning (Greedy Epsilon) on the
    Frozen Lake Game
    This function populations the empty Q matrix
    Parameters

        prior_state - int  - the prior state of the environment
        before the current timestemp
        observation - int  - the current state of the environment
        reward - int - the reward yielded from the environment
        after an action
        action - int - the action suggested by the epsilon
        greedy algorithm

    :return: None
    '''

    for episode in range(n_episodes):
        prior_state = environment.reset()
        _ = 0

        while _ < max_steps:

            if render == True: environment.render()
            action = exploit_explore(prior_state)
```

```
        observation, reward, done, info = environment.
        step(action)

        update_q_matrix(prior_state=prior_state,
                        observation=observation,
                        reward=reward,
                        action=action)

        prior_state = observation
        _ += 1

        if done:
            break

def play_frozen_lake(n_episodes):

    '''

    Directly implementing Q Learning (Greedy Epsilon) on the
    Frozen Lake Game
    This function uses the already populated Q Matrix and
    displays the game being used

    Parameters

        prior_state - int  - the prior state of the environment
        before the current timestemp
        observation - int  - the current state of the environment
        reward - int - the reward yielded from the environment
        after an action
        action - int - the action suggested by the epsilon
        greedy algorithm

    :return: None
    '''
```

```python
    for episode in range(n_episodes):
        print('Episode: %s'%episode+1)
        prior_state = environment.reset()
        done = False
        while not done:
            environment.render()
            action = choose_action(prior_state)
            observation, reward, done, info = environment.
            step(action)
            prior_state = observation
            if reward == 0:
                time.sleep(0.5)
            else:
                print('You have won on episode %s!'%(episode+1))
                time.sleep(5)
                os.system('clear')

            if done and reward == -1:
                print('You have lost this episode... :-/')
                time.sleep(5)
                os.system('clear')
                break

if __name__ == '__main__':

    populate_q_matrix(render=False)
    play_frozen_lake(n_episodes=10)
```

Doom Example

```python
import warnings, random, time, tensorflow as tf, numpy as np,
matplotlib.pyplot as plt
from neural_networks.models import DeepQNetwork
from algorithms.dql_utilities import create_environment, stack_
frames, Memory
from chapter3.frozen_lake_example import exploit_explore
from collections import deque

#Parameters
stack_size = 4
gamma = 0.95
memory_size = int(1e7)
train = True
episode_render = False
n_units = 500
n_classes = 3
learning_rate = 2e-4
stride = 4
kernel = 8
n_filters = 3
n_episodes = 1
max_steps = 100
batch_size = 64
environment, possible_actions = create_environment()
state_size = [84, 84, 4]
action_size = 3 #environment.get_avaiable_buttons_size()
explore_start = 1.0
explore_stop = 0.01
decay_rate = 1e-4
pretrain_length = batch_size
```

```python
warnings.filterwarnings('ignore')
#writer = tf.summary.FileWriter("/tensorboard/dqn/1")
write_op = tf.summary.merge_all()

def exploit_explore(session, model, explore_start, explore_
stop, decay_rate, decay_step, state, actions):
    exp_exp_tradeoff = np.random.rand()
    explore_probability = explore_stop + (explore_start -
    explore_stop) * np.exp(-decay_rate * decay_step)

    if (explore_probability > exp_exp_tradeoff):
        action = random.choice(possible_actions)

    else:
        Qs = session.run(model.output, feed_dict = {model.
        input_matrix: state.reshape((1, *state.shape))})
        choice = np.argmax(Qs)
        action = possible_actions[int(choice)]

    return action, explore_probability
def train_model(model, environment):
    tf.summary.scalar('Loss', model.error_rate)
    saver = tf.train.Saver()
    stacked_frames = deque([np.zeros((84,84), dtype=np.int) for
    i in range(stack_size)], maxlen=4)
    memory = Memory(max_size=memory_size)
    scores = []

    with tf.Session() as sess:
        sess.run(tf.global_variables_initializer())
        decay_step = 0
        environment.init()

        for episode in range(n_episodes):
```

```
step, reward_sum = 0, []
environment.new_episode()
state = environment.get_state().screen_buffer
state, stacked_frames = stack_frames(stacked_
frames, state, True)

while step < max_steps:
    step += 1; decay_step += 1

action, explore_probability = exploit_
explore(session=sess,
        model=model,
        explore_start=explore_start,
        explore_stop=explore_stop,
        decay_rate=decay_rate,
        decay_step=decay_step,
        state=state,
        actions=possible_actions)
    reward = environment.make_action(action)
    done = environment.is_episode_finished()
    reward_sum.append(reward)

    if done:

        next_state = np.zeros((84,84), dtype=np.int)

        next_state, stacked_frames = stack_
        frames(stacked_frames=stacked_frames,
        state=next_state, new_episode=False)

        step = max_steps

        total_reward = np.sum(reward_sum)

        scores.append(total_reward)
```

```
            print('Episode: {}'.format(episode),
                    'Total reward: {}'.format(total_
                    reward),
                    'Explore P: {:.4f}'.
                    format(explore_probability))

        memory.add((state, action, reward, next_
        state, done))

    else:
        next_state = environment.get_state().
        screen_buffer
        next_state, stacked_frames = stack_
        frames(stacked_frames, next_state, False)
        memory.add((state, action, reward, next_
        state, done))
        state = next_state

    batch = memory.sample(batch_size)
    states = np.array([each[0] for each in batch],
    ndmin=3)
    actions = np.array([each[1] for each in batch])
    rewards = np.array([each[2] for each in batch])
    next_states = np.array([each[3] for each in
    batch], ndmin=3)
    dones = np.array([each[4] for each in batch])
    target_Qs_batch = []

    Qs_next_state = sess.run(model.predicted_Q,
    feed_dict={model.input_matrix: next_states,
    model.actions: actions})

    for i in range(0, len(batch)):
```

```
        terminal = dones[i]

        if terminal:
            target_Qs_batch.append(rewards[i])

        else:
            target = rewards[i] + gamma *
            np.max(Qs_next_state[i])
            target_Qs_batch.append(target)

        targets = np.array([each for each in target_Qs_
        batch])

        error_rate, _ = sess.run([model.error_rate,
        model.optimizer], feed_dict={model.input_
        matrix: states, model.target_Q: targets, model.
        actions: actions})

        '''

        # Write TF Summaries
        summary = sess.run(write_op, feed_dict={model.
        inputs_: states, model.target_Q: targets,
        model.actions_: actions})

        writer.add_summary(summary, episode)
        writer.flush()

    if episode % 5 == 0:
        #saver.save(sess, filepath+'/models/model.ckpt')
        #print("Model Saved")
        '''

plt.plot(scores)
plt.title('DQN Performance During Training')
plt.xlabel('N Episodes')
```

```
    plt.ylabel('Score Value')
    plt.show()
    plt.waitforbuttonpress()
    plt.close()
    return model

def play_doom(model, environment):

    stacked_frames = deque([np.zeros((84,84), dtype=np.int) for
    i in range(stack_size)], maxlen=4)
    scores = []

    with tf.Session() as sess:

        sess.run(tf.global_variables_initializer())
        totalScore = 0

        for _ in range(100):

            done = False
            environment.new_episode()

            state = environment.get_state().screen_buffer
            state, stacked_frames = stack_frames(stacked_
            frames, state, True)

            while not environment.is_episode_finished():

                Q_matrix = sess.run(model.output, feed_dict =
                {model.input_matrix: state.reshape((1, *state.
                shape))})
                choice = np.argmax(Q_matrix)
                action = possible_actions[int(choice)]

                environment.make_action(action)
                done = environment.is_episode_finished()
                score = environment.get_total_reward()
```

```python
                scores.append(score)
                time.sleep(0.01)

                if done:
                    break

            score = environment.get_total_reward()
            print("Score: ", score)

        environment.close()

    plt.plot(scores)
    plt.title('DQN Performance After Training')
    plt.xlabel('N Episodes')
    plt.ylabel('Score Value')
    plt.show()
    plt.waitforbuttonpress()
    plt.close()

if __name__ == '__main__':

    model = DeepQNetwork(n_units=n_units,
                         n_classes=n_classes,
                         n_filters=n_filters,
                         stride=stride,
                         kernel=kernel,
                         state_size=state_size,
                         action_size=action_size,
                         learning_rate=learning_rate)

    trained_model = train_model(model=model,
                                environment=environment)

    play_doom(model=trained_model,
              environment=environment)
```

Chapter 4

Market Making Example

```
import random, tensorflow as tf, numpy as np, matplotlib.pyplot
as plt
from tgym.envs import SpreadTrading
from tgym.gens.deterministic import WavySignal
from neural_networks.market_making_models import
DeepQNetworkMM, Memory
from chapter2.cart_pole_example import calculate_discounted_
reward
from neural_networks.policy_gradient_utilities import
PolicyGradient
from tgym.gens.csvstream import CSVStreamer

#Parameters
np.random.seed(2018)
n_episodes = 1
trading_fee = .2
time_fee = 0
history_length = 2
memory_size = 2000
gamma = 0.96
epsilon_min = 0.01
batch_size = 64
action_size = len(SpreadTrading._actions)
learning_rate = 1e-2
n_layers = 4
n_units = 500
n_classes = 3
goal = 190
```

```
max_steps = 1000
explore_start = 1.0
explore_stop = 0.01
decay_rate = 1e-4
_lambda = 0.95
value_coefficient = 0.5
entropy_coefficient = 0.01
max_grad_norm = 0.5
log_interval = 10
hold = np.array([1, 0, 0])
buy = np.array([0, 1, 0])
sell = np.array([0, 0, 1])
possible_actions = [hold, buy, sell]

#Classes and variables
generator = CSVStreamer(filename='/Users/tawehbeysolow/
Downloads/amazon_order_book_data2.csv')
#generator = WavySignal(period_1=25, period_2=50, epsilon=-0.5)

memory = Memory(max_size=memory_size)

environment = SpreadTrading(spread_coefficients=[1],
                            data_generator=generator,
                            trading_fee=trading_fee,
                            time_fee=time_fee,
                            history_length=history_length)

state_size = len(environment.reset())

def baseline_model(n_actions, info, random=False):

    if random == True:
        action = np.random.choice(range(n_actions), p=np.
                repeat(1/float(n_actions), 3))
```

```python
        action = possible_actions[action]

    else:

        if len(info) == 0:
            action = np.random.choice(range(n_actions), p=np.
                    repeat(1/float(n_actions), 3))
            action = possible_actions[action]

        elif info['action'] == 'sell':
            action = buy

        else:
            action = sell

    return action

def score_model(model, n_tests):
    scores = []
    for _ in range(n_tests):
        environment.reset()
        observation = environment.reset()
        reward_sum = 0
        while True:
            "

            #environment.render()

            predict = model.predict([observation.reshape(1, 8)])[0]
            action = possible_actions[np.argmax(predict)]
            observation, reward, done, _ = environment.step(action)
            reward_sum += reward
            if done:
                break
        scores.append(reward_sum)

    return np.mean(scores)
```

```python
def exploit_explore(session, model, explore_start, explore_
stop, decay_rate, decay_step, state, actions):
    exp_exp_tradeoff = np.random.rand()
    explore_probability = explore_stop + (explore_start -
explore_stop) * np.exp(-decay_rate * decay_step)

    if (explore_probability > exp_exp_tradeoff):
        action = random.choice(possible_actions)

    else:
        Qs = session.run(model.output_layer, feed_dict =
{model.input_matrix: state.reshape((1, 8))})
        choice = np.argmax(Qs)
        action = possible_actions[int(choice)]

    return action, explore_probability

def train_model(environment, dql=None, pg=None, baseline=None):
    scores = []
    done = False
    error_rate, step = 0, 0
    info = {}
    n_episode, reward_sum, score, episode_done = 0, 0, 0, False
    n_actions = len(SpreadTrading._actions)
    observation = environment.reset()
    states = np.empty(0).reshape(0, state_size)
    actions = np.empty(0).reshape(0, len(SpreadTrading._actions))
    rewards = np.empty(0).reshape(0, 1)
    discounted_rewards = np.empty(0).reshape(0, 1)
    observation = environment.reset()

    if baseline == True:

        for episode in range(n_episodes):
```

```
    for _ in range(100):
        action = baseline_model(n_actions=n_actions,
                                info=info)

      state, reward, done, info = environment.step(action)
      reward_sum += reward

      next_state = np.zeros((state_size,), dtype=np.int)
      step = max_steps
      scores.append(reward_sum)
      memory.add((state, action, reward, next_state,
      done))

    print('Episode: {}'.format(episode),
            'Total reward: {}'.format(reward_sum))

    reward_sum = 0

  environment.reset()

  print(np.mean(scores))
  plt.hist(scores)
  plt.xlabel('Distribution of Scores')
  plt.ylabel('Relative Frequency')
  plt.show()
  plt.waitforbuttonpress()
  plt.close()

elif dql == True:

  loss = []

  model = DeepQNetworkMM(n_units=n_units,
                         n_classes=n_classes,
                         state_size=state_size,
                         action_size=action_size,
```

```
                        learning_rate=learning_rate)

#tf.summary.scalar('Loss', model.error_rate)

with tf.Session() as sess:

    sess.run(tf.global_variables_initializer())
    decay_step = 0

    for episode in range(n_episodes):

        current_step, reward_sum = 0, []
        state = np.reshape(observation, [1, state_size])

        while current_step < max_steps:

            current_step += 1; decay_step += 1

            action, explore_probability = exploit_
            explore(session=sess,
model=model,
explore_start=explore_start,
explore_stop=explore_stop,
decay_rate=decay_rate,
decay_step=decay_step,
state=state,
actions=possible_actions)

            state, reward, done, info = environment.
            step(action)
            reward_sum.append(reward)

            if current_step >= max_steps:
                done = True

            if done == True:
```

```python
            next_state = np.zeros((state_size,),
            dtype=np.int)
            step = max_steps
            total_reward = np.sum(reward_sum)
            scores.append(total_reward)
            memory.add((state, action, reward,
            next_state, done))

            print('Episode: {}'.format(episode),
                    'Total reward: {}'.
                    format(total_reward),
                    'Loss: {}'.format(error_rate),
                    'Explore P: {:.4f}'.
                    format(explore_probability))

            loss.append(error_rate)

        elif done != True:

            next_state = environment.reset()
            state = next_state
            memory.add((state, action, reward,
            next_state, done))

        batch = memory.sample(batch_size)
        states = np.array([each[0] for each in batch])
        actions = np.array([each[1] for each in batch])
        rewards = np.array([each[2] for each in batch])
        next_states = np.array([each[3] for each in
        batch])
        dones = np.array([each[4] for each in batch])

        target_Qs_batch = []
```

```python
        Qs_next_state = sess.run(model.predicted_Q,
        feed_dict={model.input_matrix: next_states,
        model.actions: actions})

        for i in range(0, len(batch)):
            terminal = dones[i]

            if terminal:
                target_Qs_batch.append(rewards[i])

            else:
                target = rewards[i] + gamma *
                np.max(Qs_next_state[i])
                target_Qs_batch.append(target)

        targets = np.array([each for each in
        target_Qs_batch])

        error_rate, _ = sess.run([model.error_rate,
        model.optimizer], feed_dict={model.input_
        matrix: states, model.target_Q: targets,
        model.actions: actions})
    if episode == n_episodes - 1:

        market_making(model=model,
                        environment=environment,
                        sess=sess,
                        state=state,
                        dpl=True)

elif pg == True:

    loss = []
```

```
mlp_model = PolicyGradient(n_units=n_units,
                           n_layers=n_layers,
                           n_columns=8,
                           n_outputs=n_classes,
                           learning_rate=learning_rate,
                           hidden_activation='selu',
                           output_activation='softmax',
                           loss_function='categorical_
                             crossentropy')

policy_model, model_predictions = mlp_model.create_
policy_model(input_shape=(len(observation), ))

policy_model.summary()

while n_episode < n_episodes:

    state = observation.reshape(1, 8)
    prediction = model_predictions.predict([state])[0]
    action = np.random.choice(range(len(SpreadTrading._
    actions)), p=prediction)
    action = possible_actions[action]
    states = np.vstack([states, state])
    actions = np.vstack([actions, action])

    observation, reward, episode_done, info =
    environment.step(action)
    reward_sum += reward
    rewards = np.vstack([rewards, reward])
    step += 1

    if step == max_steps:
        episode_done = True
```

```python
if episode_done == True:

    discounted_reward = calculate_discounted_
    reward(rewards, gamma=gamma)
    discounted_rewards = np.vstack([discounted_
    rewards, discounted_reward])

    discounted_rewards -= discounted_rewards.mean()
    discounted_rewards /= discounted_rewards.std()
    discounted_rewards = discounted_rewards.squeeze()
    actions = actions.squeeze().astype(int)

    #train_actions = np.zeros([len(actions), n_
    actions])
    #train_actions[np.arange(len(actions)),
    actions] = 1

    error = policy_model.train_on_batch([states,
    discounted_rewards], actions)
    loss.append(error)

    states = np.empty(0).reshape(0, 8)
    actions = np.empty(0).reshape(0, 3)
    rewards = np.empty(0).reshape(0, 1)
    discounted_rewards = np.empty(0).reshape(0, 1)

    score = score_model(model=model_predictions,
    n_tests=10)

    print("'\nEpisode: %s \nAverage Reward: %s  \
    nScore: %s \nError: %s"'
            )%(n_episode+1, reward_sum/float(batch_
            size), score, np.mean(loss[-batch_
            size:]))
```

```
            if score >= goal:
                break

            reward_sum = 0

            n_episode += 1
            observation = environment.reset()

        if n_episode == n_episodes - 1:

            market_making(model=model_predictions,
                          environment=environment,
                          sess=None,
                          state=state,
                          pg=True)

    if baseline != True:

        plt.title('Policy Gradient Error plot over %s
        Episodes'%(n_episode+1))
        plt.xlabel('N batches')
        plt.ylabel('Error Rate')
        plt.plot(loss)
        plt.show()
        plt.waitforbuttonpress()
        return model

def market_making(model, environment, sess, state, dpl=None,
pg=None):

    scores = []
    total_reward = 0
    environment.reset()

    for _ in range(1000):
```

```python
    for _ in range(100):

        state = np.reshape(state, [1, state_size])

        if dpl == True:
            Q_matrix = sess.run(model.output_layer, feed_dict
            = {model.input_matrix: state.reshape((1, 8))})
            choice = np.argmax(Q_matrix)
            action = possible_actions[int(choice)]

        elif pg == True:
            state = np.reshape(state, [1, 8])
            predict = model.predict([state])[0]
            action = np.argmax(predict)
            action = possible_actions[int(action)]

        state, reward, done, info = environment.step(action)
        total_reward += reward

    print('Episode: {}'.format(_),
          'Total reward: {}'.format(total_reward))
    scores.append(total_reward)
    state = environment.reset()

print(np.mean(scores))
plt.hist(scores)
plt.xlabel('Distribution of Scores')
plt.ylabel('Relative Frequency')
plt.show()
plt.waitforbuttonpress()
plt.close()

if __name__ == '__main__':

    train_model(environment=environment, dql=True)
```

Chapter 5

Sonic Example

```python
import cv2, gym, numpy as np
from retro_contest.local import make
from retro import make as make_retro
from baselines.common.atari_wrappers import FrameStack

cv2.ocl.setUseOpenCL(False)

class PreprocessFrame(gym.ObservationWrapper):
    """

    Grayscaling image from three dimensional RGB pixelated
    images
    - Set frame to gray
    - Resize the frame to 96x96x1
    """

    def __init__(self, environment, width, height):
        gym.ObservationWrapper.__init__(self, environment)
        self.width = width
        self.height = height
        self.observation_space = gym.spaces.Box(low=0,
                            high=255,shape=(self.height,
                            self.width, 1), dtype=np.
                            uint8)

    def observation(self, image):
        image = cv2.cvtColor(image, cv2.COLOR_RGB2GRAY)
        image = cv2.resize(image, (self.width, self.height),
        interpolation=cv2.INTER_AREA)
        image = image[:, :, None]
        return image
```

```python
class ActionsDiscretizer(gym.ActionWrapper):
    """

    Wrap a gym-retro environment and make it use discrete
    actions for the Sonic game.
    """

    def __init__(self, env):
        super(ActionsDiscretizer, self).__init__(env)
        buttons = ["B", "A", "MODE", "START", "UP", "DOWN",
        "LEFT", "RIGHT", "C", "Y", "X", "Z"]
        actions = [['LEFT'], ['RIGHT'], ['LEFT', 'DOWN'],
        ['RIGHT', 'DOWN'], ['DOWN'],
                    ['DOWN', 'B'], ['B']]
        self._actions = []

        """
        What we do in this loop:
        For each action in actions
            - Create an array of 12 False (12 = nb of buttons)
            For each button in action: (for instance ['LEFT'])
            we need to make that left button index = True
                - Then the button index = LEFT = True
            In fact at the end we will have an array where each
            array is an action and each elements True of this array
            are the buttons clicked.
        """

        for action in actions:
            _actions = np.array([False] * len(buttons))
            for button in action:
                _actions[buttons.index(button)] = True
            self._actions.append(_actions)
        self.action_space = gym.spaces.Discrete(len(self._actions))
```

```python
    def action(self, a):
        return self._actions[a].copy()

class RewardScaler(gym.RewardWrapper):
    """

    Bring rewards to a reasonable scale for PPO.
    This is incredibly important and effects performance
    drastically.
    """

    def reward(self, reward):

        return reward * 0.01

class AllowBacktracking(gym.Wrapper):
    """

    Use deltas in max(X) as the reward, rather than deltas
    in X. This way, agents are not discouraged too heavily
    from exploring backwards if there is no way to advance
    head-on in the level.
    """

    def __init__(self, environment):
        super(AllowBacktracking, self).__init__(environment)
        self.curent_reward = 0
        self.max_reward = 0

    def reset(self, **kwargs):
        self.current_reward = 0
        self.max_reward = 0
        return self.env.reset(**kwargs)
```

```python
    def step(self, action):
        observation, reward, done, info = self.environment.
        step(action)
        self.current_reward += reward
        reward = max(0, self.current_reward - self.max_reward)
        self.max_reward = max(self.max_reward, self.current_
        reward)
        return observation, reward, done, info

def wrap_environment(environment, n_frames=4):
    environment = ActionsDiscretizer(environment)
    environment = RewardScaler(environment)
    environment = PreprocessFrame(environment)
    environment = FrameStack(environment, n_frames)
    environment = AllowBacktracking(environment)
    return environment

def create_new_environment(environment_index, n_frames=4):
    """

    Create an environment with some standard wrappers.
    """

    dictionary = [
        {'game': 'SonicTheHedgehog-Genesis', 'state':
        'SpringYardZone.Act3'},
        {'game': 'SonicTheHedgehog-Genesis', 'state':
        'SpringYardZone.Act2'},
        {'game': 'SonicTheHedgehog-Genesis', 'state':
        'GreenHillZone.Act3'},
        {'game': 'SonicTheHedgehog-Genesis', 'state':
        'GreenHillZone.Act1'},
        {'game': 'SonicTheHedgehog-Genesis', 'state':
        'StarLightZone.Act2'},
```

```python
        {'game': 'SonicTheHedgehog-Genesis', 'state':
        'StarLightZone.Act1'},
        {'game': 'SonicTheHedgehog-Genesis', 'state':
        'MarbleZone.Act2'},
        {'game': 'SonicTheHedgehog-Genesis', 'state':
        'MarbleZone.Act1'},
        {'game': 'SonicTheHedgehog-Genesis', 'state':
        'MarbleZone.Act3'},
        {'game': 'SonicTheHedgehog-Genesis', 'state':
        'ScrapBrainZone.Act2'},
        {'game': 'SonicTheHedgehog-Genesis', 'state':
        'LabyrinthZone.Act2'},
        {'game': 'SonicTheHedgehog-Genesis', 'state':
        'LabyrinthZone.Act1'},
        {'game': 'SonicTheHedgehog-Genesis', 'state':
        'LabyrinthZone.Act3'}]

    print(dictionary[environment_index]['game'])
    print(dictionary[environment_index]['state'])

    environment = make(game=dictionary[environment_index]['game'],
                   state=dictionary[environment_index]['state'],
                   bk2dir="./records")

    environment = wrap_environment(environment=environment,
                                 n_frames=n_frames)

    return environment
def make_test_level_Green():
    return make_test()
```

```python
def make_test(n_frames=4):
    """

    Create an environment with some standard wrappers.
    """

    environment = make_retro(game='SonicTheHedgehog-Genesis',
                             state='GreenHillZone.Act2',
                             record="./records")

    environment = wrap_environment(environment=environment,
                                   n_frames=n_frames)

    return environment
```

Index

A

Actor advantage critic (A2C), 11,
    38, 47
Actor-Critic model, 11, 37, 103
    advantage function, 37
    A2C, 38
    A3C, 38
Artificial intelligence, 5, 19
Asynchronous advantage
    Actor-Critic (A3C), 11, 38, 47

B

baseline_model() function, 88

C

calculate_discounted_reward()
    function, 30
Cart Pole game, 125–129
Cart Pole problem
    cart_pole_game(), 27
    environment_dimension
        variable, 27
    Keras, 25
    neural network, 26, 27
    probabilities, 28

coord.join() function, 111
Credit-assignment problem
    (cap), 5
Custom OpenAI
    A3C Actor-Critic
        dynamic run() function, 107
        LSTM model, 106
        main/master function,
          108, 109
        model() class, 104
        visualization, 103
        worker.work() function,
          109, 110
    download game
        commands, 98
        steam dashboard, 97
    environment code
        actions, 102
        ActionsDiscretizer(), 101
        AllowBacktracting() class,
          102, 103
        body function, 98
        observationWrapper
          class, 100
        retro_contest" module,
          99, 100
    Sonic the Hedgehog, 95, 96

© Taweh Beysolow II 2019
T. Beysolow II, *Applied Reinforcement Learning with Python*,
https://doi.org/10.1007/978-1-4842-5127-0

Printed in the United States
By Bookmasters